AT HOME ABROAD

Today's Expats Tell Their Stories

Compiled & Edited by
Betsy & Mark Blondin

At Home Abroad
Today's Expats Tell Their Stories

Expat Expressions
©2016 by Word Metro Press

United States of America

All rights reserved.

ISBN: 978-0-9886228-1-4

First Edition

Compiled and edited by Betsy and Mark Blondin

Cover design by Mark Blondin

Editor's Note: We decided to retain the American and British English spellings and punctuation of the authors, so please forgive any inconsistencies.

MERRY CHRISTMAS
KG —
TRAVELING IS GOOD
FOR THE SOUL
AND NOW YOU HAVE
THE TIME !!. Love
DP & Jo

Dedication

This collection is dedicated
to our children, Donald, Kelly
and Stacy, who have embraced
our unconventional lifestyle.

Acknowledgments

As always, we thank our families
and friends for their support and
encouragement. We applaud
our authors and treasure their
contributions. A special note of
appreciation goes to Jean White
for her valuable editing and design
advice, and to Donna Baxter
for tons of loving feedback.

Contents

7 INTRODUCTION

13 SURPRISES IN ISTANBUL
Alba Brunetti: From New York to Istanbul, a woman finds
herself, home and surprises in an amazing place

19 LIFE IN JAPAN
John Hartman: An expat from the US with a sense of humor
thrives in Japan

27 WHY I LIVE IN GUATEMALA
Maria Emilia Martin: An accomplished Latina journalist from
the US making a difference in Central America

33 EXPATS IN CAMBODIA
Frank and Gabrielle Yetter:
Two journalists move to Cambodia and never turn back

43 FOUND IN BUENOS AIRES
Jerry Nelson: A worldly photojournalist who knows adventure
finds love and life in Buenos Aires

53 A POLISH GIRL WHO HAD A DREAM
Barbara Galewska: A Polish girl with a dream lives it in Brazil

59 GROWING UP IN BARCELONA
Nia Evans: Our youngest expat reflects on moving from London
and life in Barcelona

65 THE EMOTIONAL ROLLERCOASTER THAT IS EXPAT LIFE
Els Mahieu: From Belgium, a woman traveler discovers herself
and life in Belfast

71 DISCOVERY
Rebecca Conklin: A full circle of discovery
from the US to Shanghai and back

77 MOVING TO MEDELLÍN
Lisa Imogen Eldridge: Surprised to find her British heart in
Medellin, Colombia, after traveling the world

81 It's Easy to Fall in Love with Life in Thailand!
Laura Gibbs: A young English woman's practical guide
to life in Thailand

87 Cultural Reciprocity & the True Meaning of "Home"
Jessica Beder: From the US to Buenos Aires,
a young woman's journey

99 Living the Good Life in Panama
Terry Coles: A couple retires early and embraces
a laid-back life in Panama

109 The Thousand-Year Crawl
Taylor Bell: A creative reflection of this young teacher's life
in Madrid

115 Belgian Footprints
Any Brasó: After tasting life in Toronto, a woman from Spain
finds home, friends and peace in Brussels

125 An Expat Woman in Greece
Rebecca Hall: A woman from the UK falls under the magic spell
of Greece

131 At the Heart of It
Kaleena Stroud: A young woman's tale of travel and finding her
life in Buenos Aires

137 A Second Life: Full Circle
Tamás Inczédy: From Hungary he travels to Indonesia and back
again to find home and family

141 The Journey Here
Ed O'Connor: Disillusioned with the US, this retiree invents a
lifestyle in Cuenca, Ecuador

149 Abroad in Argentina
Stephen Siefert: A one-legged pigeon helps a young man from
Oregon appreciate his life in Buenos Aires

155 This Old World Is a New World
Michael Sinding: From Canada to Europe, this couple explores
Austria, The Netherlands and Germany

169 Dutch in Portugal

Wim Minten: Growing up in Holland, he felt out of place but found happiness in travel and life in Portugal

179 An Expat Story – Moving to Morocco

Tristan Morton-Clark: Finding love in Marrakesh, loving life in England and realizing retirement dreams in Morocco

185 How in the Hell Did This Happen?

Jackie Gambill: A pre-retirement couple leaves their comfort zone to travel and house-sit abroad

191 From Oaxaca to LA

Soraya Heydari: A young woman from England explores Oaxaca, Mexico, then settles in Los Angeles

197 The Main Reason I'm Here

Susan Schenck: Cuenca ruins her marriage, but this woman from California finds her paradise in Ecuador

203 Medellín

Ryan Hiraki: Never dreaming he would settle outside the US, this young man from Hawaii lives in Colombia

213 Intentionality with Flexibility

Susan and Richard Neulist: Retirees from the northeastern US living a fluid life in San Miguel de Allende, Mexico

221 Living in Costa Rica

Judith Donovan: Costa Rica offers this couple a place for their dream home and continuing adventures

231 A Shattered Field of Dreams?

Alvin Starkman, M.A., J.D.: A Canadian lawyer finds new passion in Oaxaca

241 Musings from the Monastery

Earl Goodson: One question motivates this young man from the US to experience life in New Zealand and Taiwan

246 Expat Resources

Introduction

Over the last six years we have lived in Europe, South and Central America, and Mexico. Part of our journey's magic involves meeting fascinating people who have left their home countries in pursuit of something difficult to define or articulate. The stories they tell have impressed and inspired us. What makes expats different? Why and how do they give up the comforts of home, family and community in search of something else? Why does one person jump into a lifestyle that others only dream of?

Adventure. Discovery. Love. Career. Finances. Disenchantment. Retirement. These are the primary motivations for people who move and live abroad, far from their home country, family and friends. Whatever their reasons, they are the new expats.

What is an expat, anyway? For this collection we decided to set aside various words and the definitions of emigrant, immigrant, expatriate, émigré, world traveler, adventure seeker and the like, and simply use "expat." Many people consider the term in the historical context of famous expatriates, such as John Steinbeck, Ernest Hemmingway, Ezra Pound,

Gertrude Stein, F. Scott Fitzgerald, T.S. Eliot, Isadora Duncan — those who sought inspiration, a collective cultural experience, or an alternative to what they saw as a stale experience at home. Certainly that strain exists today. But the world of today's expats is much richer.

In her story in this book, Rebecca Hall says simply: "What is an expat? I know the dictionary definition: 'To withdraw oneself from residence in one's native country.'" And for this book, we decided to stick with that.

Variations of the expat experience have grown to include untethered workers, those working for multinational corporations, retirees seeking adventure or a lower cost of living, and those filled with wanderlust or love and romance. In addition we include people who are slow travelers, living in each place for an extended time in order to discover more about it and its culture. Slow travel, with or without a home base, has become a part of the expat experience.

Certainly, easy travel and global connections have enabled this larger group of expats. The Internet makes it much easier to plan and book travel, find information for destinations, and stay in touch with family and friends via phone, online chats and social media.

Sometimes it's as simple as someone taking a vacation, falling in love with a place or its people and deciding to buy a house and stay. People move about, meet others and find amazing places that become new homes.

Expats have in common the ability to abandon the familiar and leap into an unknown future. For some it happens by a series of coincidences, for others it's well-planned. And for some, like retirees moving abroad, it's born from necessity. This is not to say we can pigeonhole each type, and from our experience there is overlap. We think you will find common threads.

Looking at the numbers and countries provides insight into how large and diverse this movement has become and how little of it we understand. Several expat surveys and resources exist, and we include their links in the back of the book.

There is no agreement on the number of expats worldwide. Estimates range from 50 million to more than 230 million. The discrepancies might be found in the definition of an expat and the difficulty of quantifying the phenomenon. But no one disputes that the numbers are growing rapidly.

For example, the US Department of State estimates that one million US citizens live in Mexico, and that eight million live and work around the globe. According to the Association of American Residents Overseas (AARO), those eight million (excluding military) live in 160-plus countries.

Three expat surveys provide useful information for those inspired by these stories or on the verge of testing the expat waters. Expat Insider is a worldwide survey by InterNations with 14,000 respondents in 195 countries and territories. The Expat Survey and its Expat Media Hub provide valuable information and statistics for expats everywhere. HSBC's Expat Explorer Global Report is in its eighth year as one of these comprehensive surveys.

The AARO was founded in 1973 and has members in 46 countries. It researches and informs members about issues affecting the lives of Americans overseas. The *Wall Street Journal* has an expat section and Facebook page, and *The Huffington Post* features many expat stories. A wealth of information is available for all expats, current and future.

In the US, becoming an expat and leaving to live in another country is viewed by some as almost traitorous. Why would anyone leave the "greatest, most exceptional country in history"? Yet strong forces including love, money and adventure push people to leave home and embark on uncertain journeys.

We were not sure what drives the movement in other countries, and that makes some of these stories both revealing and confirming. We began this project expecting to hear primarily from retirees in popular expat locations and ended up with narratives from people of all ages and lifestyles in many countries. Similar themes arise.

Our stories include some from expats who have returned home permanently or for part of the year. We retained their essays because they too have become part of the global expat experience.

In addition to "expat," we wanted to define the word "home" for this book. As we move about, we often say we carry home with us in our hearts or suitcases, or simply that home is wherever we are.

In her essay, Susan Neulist says, "Our lives have been richer since moving from our home country. Now we would find it hard to decide what that home country would be, as 'home' has become the place we are in at the moment."

Jessica Beder says, "Suddenly home is not just the place you live. Home is the piece of your soul that finds its counterpoint in the intoxication of cultural reciprocity."

And in his narrative, Earl Goodson says, "I will return and I will go, but home is wherever I can find a moment to be still and ask, 'Why?' "

Whatever your definition of expat or home, the following stories represent a mosaic of people who have chosen or tasted the expat lifestyle. We chose to place the essays in random order rather than by category, geography or author's age, so you will see how and where the themes overlap — and the ways in which we are the same no matter where we come from or where we're going.

This isn't the final picture of today's expats, or even a complete one, but we hope you find some answers, a broader perspective and some inspiration. We live in exciting times, ever more connected, with myriad options in a world beyond what previous generations could have imagined.

See the world through the eyes of these expats. Enjoy the journey, and the magic.

Betsy and Mark Blondin
March 2016

"America is my country and
Paris is my hometown."
— Gertrude Stein

Surprises in Istanbul

Alba Brunetti

There's an old saw about New Yorkers that they always say they want to leave the city but never do. I know that leaving what was familiar — and not altogether comfortable — was very hard for me. I had been saying I wanted to leave New York for 10 years and could not bring myself to do anything about it. Over that 10-year period, bit by bit the evidence gathered and pointed me to another life. But I didn't know what that life was until I came to it. I had grown up in New York, been educated at the best schools and had worked there for almost 20 years. But I wasn't happy.

I was tired of the high pressure and highly insecure Internet jobs I had. On the one hand, I always loved cutting-edge ideas and new experiences. On the other hand, I was disappointed that I never had the economic security I craved. Not the routine, mind you, I was in a very strict routine that revolved around my work but as the years passed, nothing in my life really changed and nothing interested me or excited me anymore about New York. Yes, I know it's one of the world's most exciting cities. It was also a city I knew too well and for someone as creative as I am, that did not bode well. I knew I needed something new. The turning point happened when my father died. That's when I knew that I had passed the midpoint of my life — if I were going to have the good fortune of living as long as he had. I had to face the cold hard truth that I wasn't happy and the only way out was to change something, anything or everything. I chose the latter.

A few things worked in my favor. I'm single, so I didn't have to ask anyone else's opinion. I had also been an expat in my 20s living in Italy where I had extended family. I saw the writing on the wall at my job, so it was somewhat easy to cut my losses and try something really new. Lastly and perhaps most importantly, I had a dream to write a book and I was halfway through it and wanted to give myself the time and the space to finish it.

I initially set off for Italy for three months. Somewhere in the back of my mind I had the desire to remain, though I couldn't really admit it to myself. I was desperately unhappy there too — Italy held no surprises for me either and was not the best place for the peace and quiet I needed to finish my book. Right before my three-month stay was drawing to a close, by serendipity and chance, I visited two friends from New York who were living in Istanbul. Even before my plane landed, I knew something important was happening. I didn't know it right away, but I had found my new home. I finished my first book and had also found a new and exciting city in which to live.

Let's say it was a big surprise. I had always thought I would end up in a very small town or in the countryside after living in New York City. In fact, all my fantasies about expat life involved slowing down and country cottages with gardens and rolling hills. Nothing was more surprising to me or my friends than my moving to a city even bigger than New York. Hadn't I wanted peace and quiet? Well, I was open to surprises — in fact, I was specifically looking to be surprised.

And I was. I was surprised how instantly I became a part of Turkish culture. It was easy to feel at home because everyone was so welcoming and kind to me. I chose to live in a regular neighborhood instead of an expat neighborhood. This made all the difference; I felt like a long-lost daughter and not just another visitor, which is the way expat neighborhoods often make you feel. Everyone went out of their way to help me and they still do, as my Turkish language skills are mostly food-based. I'm lucky because English is common here and most young people speak it well. I've put on many delicious pounds and don't regret any of them. Sometimes I miss a good old slice of New York pizza, but there are many wonderful substitutes here. Every region of Turkey is well represented in Istanbul's culinary offerings. I enjoy discovering the new flavors of my new home, most especially if it is home cooking.

Istanbul is home to over 12 million people. It is known as the city where East meets West. Half of it is located on the European continent and the other half is on the Asian continent. It is separated by the Bosphorus Strait, which is a mesmerizing body of water. Locals routinely ferry across it, often criss-crossing the continents for work and home. I find

Istanbul to be an intoxicating blend of many old-world cultures — with something wonderfully and exotically all its own. In some very interesting ways, I feel I have become part of that mix.

Taking a Western perspective, I would say that having a plan to be an expat is an easier and more secure way of moving to a different country. Having a job lined up with the amenities that an 'expat package' offers gives one more security and answers a lot of life's questions beforehand. But if you are like me and feel the call of adventure and surprise, it is also doable — though not as secure. I like to think the way I ended up in Istanbul was a very 'Eastern' way, having been drawn somewhere without a real plan, but with some longing or knowing in my heart and then watching it all unfold.

As a writer and freelancer, I've kept my US bank account as well as my connections to the US (and the English-speaking market) strong. I write in English, so keeping ties with my New York friends and certain aspects of my New York life is crucial. That doesn't mean that I am not also rooted here in Istanbul. I have a residency permit that is renewed yearly, a Turkish bank account and a Turkish tax ID. There was some bureaucracy involved in getting my residency permit, but the laws have changed since then and the requirements are now also available online. Both the Turkish bank account and tax ID were relatively easy to acquire, though the high number of signatures involved in getting the bank account became a comedy routine in which paper after paper required my signature or initials.

The most challenging experiences I have had have been around work — especially since I have not had a full-time job and have freelanced since my arrival. I have found working with individual Turkish people to be wonderful. Communication runs quite smoothly and payment is easy and involves money transfers to my account. My experiences with larger companies, even global ones, however, much less so. Concepts of professionalism are quite different and often challenging to navigate as a freelancer.

There are opportunities in Turkey for all types of work, but especially for English teachers. Most schools, however, are looking for certifications. Get those before you come to make the process easier. Also, there are many online groups, especially on Facebook, that post teaching opportunities in Istanbul as well as all over Turkey. If your job offers the possibility of working remotely, Istanbul is an ideal place to enjoy a new culture and high quality of life.

I'm happy here in this city that never ceases to surprise and amaze me. As a writer, I find Istanbul to be a fascinating subject. The grandeur, the beauty and the charm are infinite and always changing. The country of Turkey is a treasure trove of history stretching back millennia with links not only to the Abrahamic faiths, but also to ancient civilizations that puzzle archeologists to this day. Although I knew some aspects of the cultural richness and heritages, it's only since I have lived here that I discovered I had known only the tip of the iceberg.

Finding your right place or your new home is like falling in love. You'll know it when you find it. And it can happen at any age or any time of life. In fact,

I found it that much sweeter that I discovered my new home in my 40s. Whatever age or stage of life, becoming an expat is a wonderful and life-affirming adventure. It opens you up to a world of possibilities and I do mean *world*. I cannot deny that there have been challenges but the rewards have been plentiful too. Most importantly, I find I am finally living the life I always dreamed. I wish you all the best in finding your new home, whenever you are ready and wherever that might be.

Alba Brunetti
US / Istanbul, Turkey

Alba Brunetti was born in Italy and grew up in New York City. She worked for many years in New Media before moving to Istanbul. She has a column on The Huffington Post *as well as a blog,* The Bluest I.

Life in Japan

John Hartman

When people find out I live in Japan, they often say something along the lines of, "Wow, I wish I could do that."

To which I respond: "Why don't you?"

Okay, that's not entirely true. What I *usually* say are things like, "How can you people from Chase Bank keep finding me?" and, "No, I'm not sure which of my exes filed for the cash settlement," and, "Of course I'm not living under an assumed name, Mom; 'Geraldine Swanson' is the way my name is pronounced in Japanese."

That's not entirely true, either. But I do live in Japan and have, off and on since 2003.

Let me get the most important advice out of the way first: *All McDonald's and Starbucks in Japan have Western-style toilets.* That might not seem vital to you now but trust me, the very instant it does become critical, you're going to thank me for knowing that. You're welcome.

I ran a delivery service in Seattle in 1999, dealing with customers who needed things delivered across town quickly, who wanted to know why things hadn't been delivered yet, who wanted to know if their things were *ever* going to be delivered, and who wanted to complain about our bicycle messengers.

"They track dirt across our stone floors," they said.

"Don't track dirt across the stone floors," I told the messengers.

"Their radios are too loud when they are in our offices."

"Can you guys turn the radios down a bit when you go into the drop? Thanks."

"Your guys look kind of scruffy. Can't they wear helmets and uniforms?"

"Guys, can you wear the T-shirts we give you? Also, we gave you money to buy helmets. Please wear helmets."

"Ha, we're not wearing helmets," the bike messengers said. "Helmets aren't safe."

I couldn't force them to wear helmets. They weren't required by law.

Then one afternoon one of the messengers, on his last delivery of the day, took a corner and was hit head-on by an SUV going way too fast.

I didn't know this messenger, but I was introduced to his father at his funeral a few days later.

A few days after that, I walked into the office of the company's owner.

"I'm gonna take three weeks off."

"Good idea," he said.

"At Christmas."

"Sure. Going anywhere interesting?"

"Japan," I said, without really thinking about it.

Japan is like living in an alternate universe: everything is reasonably familiar, right up to the point where it isn't. You see Nikes and Burger King and KFC and baseball and Toyota Priuses and lull yourself into a false sense of security until you can't find shoes in your size *anywhere* and you discover Burger King sells, no kidding, black burgers with black buns and black sauce, and KFC is where you take your date for dinner on Christmas Eve and holy smokes, the Priuses are driving on the *wrong* side of the road.

When I reached Kyoto, the differences were already starting to get to me. I had been in Tokyo for a few days experiencing the magic and wonder of Christmas (spoiler alert: there is none). I had been to Nara where a deer tried to eat my passport (there is a sentence that will earn you a trip to the Government Special Conversation Room at the airport when you return home). I had been to Osaka where I had mostly been sick, and I had been to Hiroshima where a Pakistani student tried to start a fight with me, ironically in front of the Peace Museum.

So I was a little twitchy when I got off the Shinkansen at Kyoto Station and looked around at the tree-covered hills surrounding the place, saw the endless temples and shrines, and felt the calm pace of the place. One word, unbidden, crossed my mind: "Yes." The twitchiness vanished. That evening was New Year's Eve. I found a British pub downtown. For some reason, the Japanese love British-style pubs, and they really love Irish pubs. Kyoto has six or seven Irish pubs in a city of one and a half million people. I'm reasonably sure that I know every actual Irish person in Kyoto, and there's one pub for each of them.

In this pub there were darts and beer and Crazy Dave, a 50-year-old ex-Marine with a cowboy shirt and a Stevie Ray Vaughan hat, who had been living and working in Kyoto for 10 years. Crazy Dave is Kyoto's No. 1 fan. "This place is really great!" I shouted as we toasted the new year with a traditional British beer while Japanese pop music blared over the speakers. "I know!" shouted Crazy Dave. "I mean, this place is *really* awesome," I continued. "Yeah," said Crazy Dave, "You should totally move here."

In a second *everything changed.* Up to that point, I had thought about my life in terms of limitations. I couldn't do this. I could never be that. This was never going to happen. But sitting there across from an insane ex-hippie from Virginia I worked it out. I want to do X. Other people do X. I am a person. Therefore, I can do X.

"Good idea," I told Dave, then returned to America, sold my motorcycle and pickup truck, and moved to Kyoto. Again, that part's not entirely true. At least it didn't happen that fast. It took about another 18 months of tidying up affairs, selling stuff, quitting the old job, getting a new job because I quit the old one too soon, buying tickets, and so forth.

Also, the way I did it the first time was kind of stupid, in that I didn't really have any sort of plan. I arranged online for a room in a guesthouse, a sort of boarding house with a private room and a mini-fridge. This particular guesthouse was run by a very nice man who completely failed to note in any of our correspondence that the shared shower (100 yen for 15 minutes of hot water) was right in the middle of the shared kitchen. As in, somebody installed a shower stall *right smack dab in the middle of the shared kitchen.* This made for some interesting encounters. The guesthouse also had only Japanese-style toilets, which are perfectly sanitary and easy to use, except that the first step in the process is to "remove every item of clothing below the waist."

Believe it or not, though, that was the *smart* part of my moving to Japan. I didn't speak the language. I knew three people in the whole country. I had no job. I was on a 90-day tourist visa, which meant I couldn't get a job, a bank account, or a proper cell phone. My only Internet access was at an Internet café a mile away. And back then I smoked, which is as much of a drain on the cash flow there as it is in the States.

I found a local foreigner newsletter and started looking for work. Surprisingly, I was hired right away, and "right away" means "please wait three weeks for your paperwork to arrive from the US, then four weeks for your visa to be changed to the correct type, and then another two months before receiving your first real paycheck."

After working there about five years, augmenting my income by singing in Kyoto bars and nightclubs, the company I worked for imploded in spectacular fashion. I moved back to the States just in time for the Great Recession and was lucky to get a job driving big rigs all over North America, until, at the age of 48, I decided to go back to college. I did two years of school in Seattle and was accepted to a university in Tokyo, where I currently live on a student visa.

So, what have I learned about life as an expat? Here's a short list.

Bring money, but don't let a lack of it hold you back. People always say, "Oh, Japan is so expensive.

I took a cab from the airport to my hotel in Tokyo and it was a hundred dollars!" Yeah, lady, if you took a cab from the Hamptons to Kennedy Airport, it would be expensive, too. It's 70 kilometers from New Tokyo International Airport, which isn't even in Tokyo, to downtown Tokyo. Take the train instead; trains are cheap. Got a lot of luggage? There's a service at the airport that will deliver it to your hotel. Can't afford expensive restaurants? Neither can Tokyo cab drivers; ask yours where he likes to eat and go there for a cheap meal. Or just buy food from one of the estimated eleventy-zillion convenience stores in the city. Remember, if it were too expensive to live there, it wouldn't be so crowded.

Problems always have a solution if you're creative. The trains in Japan generally stop running around midnight; no one knows why. Maybe the cab drivers and train companies do some price-fixing. I got stuck downtown late one night with not enough money for a cab and two or three hours to kill until the trains started again. It was winter and cold, so I didn't want to just walk around outside. Fortunately, I spotted a 24-hour manga café. These are places where for an hourly fee you can sit and borrow as many Japanese comics as you like, sit in a big comfortable recliner and read to your heart's content. Or you can carefully select a largish book and place it over your face, lean back in the recliner, set the alarm on your phone to go off in a few hours, and conk out. Some cafes have private cubicles for Internet access, with couches, and the owners don't care if you read or not, because they're getting their hourly fee. Some late-night folks go into a 24-hour McDonalds, buy a cheap cup of coffee, find a table upstairs, and zonk out.

The things you will miss are not the things you expect. I am currently experiencing an existential crisis brought on by a severe lack of Huy Fong Sriracha sauce in my life. It never occurred to me that there would be no sriracha here; I am from Seattle where every restaurant has a bottle of the stuff on the table and there are huge displays of it in the aisles at Safeway. They sell a lame, over-processed version of sriracha here, but it's not the same. Similarly, tortillas are not impossible to find. In fact they are in most grocery stores here but they're kind of expensive. So get used to either doing without, making your own (I make a pretty good hummus these days, for example), or paying extra at an import store.

Some years ago I returned to Seattle for a visit, and my sister picked me up at the airport. On the way home we stopped at the grocery store where I purchased a loaf of whole wheat bread, a bottle of yellow mustard, a package of Tillamook sharp cheddar, a package of Oscar Meyer bologna, and a 12-pack of Mountain Dew. I'm not proud to admit that.

Finally, and this is may be the most important, *nobody here knows you.* Unless you travel with your family, of course. But this is a chance to be the you you've always wanted to be. This is your Big International Adventure. Grab that opportunity with both hands. Walk up the street you would usually avoid. Eat the food that smells great but you don't know exactly what it is. Oh, wait, except something called *nankotsu.* That is deep-fried chicken cartilage.

It looks great, smells great, and is like trying to eat the ring on the back of a baby's pacifier. So skip that.

Go into the shops. Ask what that thing on the wall with the weird handle and the wicker-looking paddle is for. *Talk to the people.* Absolutely talk to the people. You don't have to be rude or intrusive, just ask them if they have always lived in this neighborhood. Ask them if they know a good cheap place to eat, or an interesting gallery, or someplace nice to take the kids, or a great place to hear some live music. Anything, but talk to them. Don't be embarrassed; who knows you here?

Because this is the thing: when I was a kid, we would drive across the country on vacation, from Seattle to visit my dad's family in Indiana. We drove through towns and cities and I thought about the houses. I wondered: *Who lives there? What sort of work do they do? Are they happy? Are they nice?*

Then I got older and traveled and met other people, and it turned out those other people wondered the same thing about me, and some of them became friends.

And that's the key: We're just not all that different from one another.

So get out there. Have an adventure. The planet is too big and interesting not to see some of it while you're here.

Remember that thing about the toilets, though.

John Hartman
Age 51
US / Tokyo, Japan

Why I Live in Guatemala

Maria Emilia Martin

I live in Guatemala because each day I wake up and see the volcano called Agua out my window. As the day goes on, the volcano changes before my eyes: first it's clear against a blue sky, then the clouds roll in and I see only the top of the cone, and then it's totally covered by mist and clouds. By evening, it may reappear. It's almost like a point of focus for meditation, a lesson in mindfulness. I watch the volcano out the picture window facing the desk where I do my work: my computer keeping me in touch with the rest of the world, Agua bringing me back to the here and now.

I first visited this Central American country in 1975 and fell in love. Guatemala is one of the most beautiful places I've seen. Within its borders are pristine rainforest, monumental ancient Mayan cities, and what Aldous Huxley called the most beautiful lake in the world, the majestic and mysterious Atitlan. Almost 30 years later, I returned on a Fulbright scholarship to work with indigenous radio stations. When it was time to leave, I just couldn't do it.

Somehow, Guatemala feels like home to me. Home is where I've found balance and a healing sanctuary; home is where it's okay not to do anything at all every once in a while; home is where I often go to sleep by eight in the evening — something absolutely unheard of in my former life.

In my former life, I worked 12-plus-hour days; in my former life I was "important"; in my former life I was my work. Here I'm the person who lives and works and meditates and sometimes tries to write, and no one really knows about it. And that's just fine.

In this life, a simple morning greeting from Don Santos, the gardener, brings a golden light of joy lasting the whole day. An exchange at the laundry or the corner store can be an exquisitely sweet encounter.

> *"Still, for me it's not enough to come for the cheaper living and spring-like climate. To truly enjoy all the benefits of being here while coping with the disadvantages, I personally feel I have to give back to this country."*

Not everything in Guatemala is sweet of course. "One of the most violent countries in the world" is how the European Union recently characterized this place I now call home. And if you take a look at the State Department's Consular Report on Guatemala, it may make you run for your life. "Violent criminal activity has been a problem in all parts of Guatemala for years, including murder, rape, and armed assaults against foreigners" is how it starts, and it gets more frightening as the details emerge.

One of these details is that Guatemala is a developing country attempting to rise from one of the longest civil wars in the hemisphere — almost four decades of conflict that ran from 1954 (when the United States helped overthrow the democratically elected government of Jacobo Arbenz) to 1996 when peace accords ended the bloody war that had killed over 200,000 Guatemalans.

Nearly 20 years after the official end of the war, the country is still awash with guns. Unemployment and underemployment are high, and literacy is low. Governments, even in this "new democracy," have been to one extent or another corrupt and have neglected social ills.

In this country just about the size of Tennessee, the reality of poverty, illness, crime, and the disparity between the rich and the poor is never far away. In effect, what exists in Guatemala is a situation much like a great deal of this world. Although I certainly don't like the inequality, living here makes me feel closer to reality, more alive, more in tune with the majority of humanity. Viewing poverty on a regular basis, I feel more grateful for what I have.

In the States, it's often too easy to believe that we are what the rest of the world is like, too easy to fall into a cocoon of comfort, materialism, and denial — to forget how lucky we are. Even for those with means, living in Guatemala is to some extent uncomfortable. I don't often go out past dark; I almost never take public transportation; I hardly ever drive by myself and certainly never at night.

There are huge contradictions here. They stare you in the face: such a warm sweet people, so much death and violence. The legacy of the war is still felt in the random street crime; people are killed for cell phones and bicycles.

Here, my mobility is limited. Or, I limit my mobility. But in the need to make my world smaller, that smaller world is somehow richer. I'm more relaxed, more at home in my home, more in tune to what I need, more... yes, "balanced."

"Do you have many friends there?" people ask. Not really — my work often takes me to the rural areas outside of Antigua and into the gritty capital, Guatemala City. Still, wherever I am in this country, I feel more human warmth on a day-to-day basis than on an average day in my life in *el Norte*.

These days, I see many more baby boomer-aged Americans on the streets of Antigua. I think they too have discovered the economic advantages of being here. Rent is relatively cheaper as are some food prices, and foreigners can usually afford help.

My Antigua hideaway (most houses here are located behind high walls and thick wooden gates) was even more appealing after I suffered a health crisis and needed time and a place to heal. This was one place I could afford not to take on a full-time job for a while.

Still, for me it's not enough to come for the cheaper living and spring-like climate. To truly enjoy all the benefits of being here while coping with the disadvantages, I personally feel I have to give back to this country.

Countless Americans and other internationals are here doing just that: working in clinics, establishing NGOs for reproductive health, literacy, or micro-lending; or like me, working with rural and indigenous journalists. In doing this, I think we take part in the process of trying to establish a different relationship with the people of Guatemala than that which has been traditional for so long: Here come the gringos to plunder and profit — and off they go somewhere else when a better opportunity opens up.

Maria Emilia Martin
US / Antiqua, Guatemala

María Emilia Martin is a pioneering public radio journalist with over two dozen awards for her work covering Latino issues and Latin America. She has developed ground-breaking programs and series for public radio, including NPR's Latino USA, *and* Despues de las Guerras: Central America After the Wars. *She currently heads the GraciasVida Center for Media, training rural and indigenous journalists in Guatemala and Bolivia.*

"It is a bittersweet thing, knowing two cultures. Once you leave your birthplace, nothing is ever the same."
— Sarah Turnbull

Expats in Cambodia

Frank (Skip) and Gabrielle (Gabi) Yetter

Our love affair with Southeast Asia began in 2007 when my husband, Skip, and I honeymooned in Thailand, and our two-week trip turned into a journey that changed our lives. We fell in love with the gentleness, warmth and spirituality of the people and decided we wanted to experience more, so we launched ourselves us on a quest to move there.

Up to this point, we hadn't planned on leaving the US but once we returned home to Marblehead, Massachusetts, a seed had been planted and quickly taken root. Although we'd been happy in this lovely little seaside town, we acknowledged we wanted something different. We were ready to break away from traditional lifestyles, cut loose from the bonds of consumerism and ownership and launch ourselves into the unknown.

So our days took on a different focus. Before going into work, Skip spent most of his early morning hours on the Internet, searching for places, ideas and opportunities for us to move to Southeast Asia and instead of planning another vacation, we focused on leaving.

Our first step was to sell our house (at a loss), get rid of most of our possessions and downsize to a small condo in preparation for the time when we'd be able to go. After researching, talking, planning and exploring for the next two years, we found the answer: VIA (Volunteers in Asia). We applied online, were interviewed by the programme directors of this small volunteer organisation that placed people in positions throughout Southeast Asia and a couple of weeks later were offered posts working with NGOs in Phnom Penh.

Neither of us knew much about Cambodia but we were keen to find out.

So began the process of elimination and change. We sold our cars, found a home for our cat, Gracie, and sold or gave away most of our stuff. Skip quit his job in January 2010, I closed down my home business and in June 2010 we found ourselves at the Boston airport with a one-way ticket to Phnom Penh.

It was a new adventure for both of us and as we said farewell to friends and family, neither of us had any idea when — or if — we'd be back.

For Skip it meant extricating himself from a lifetime of living in Massachusetts. He'd raised two daughters (the youngest of whom finished college the year we left), run newspapers throughout the state and worked in a high-profile job as Senior Vice President of Business Wire (a global newswire company). His roots ran deep and there was plenty to untangle.

I, on the other hand, had spent most of my life moving around the world. I was raised in Bahrain (the daughter of a British mother and Maltese father), worked as a journalist in South Africa and had travelled extensively since I was a child. In 1982 I travelled to the US on a vacation from which I never returned. Skip and I met when we both worked at Business Wire, a global newswire service based in San Francisco. He ran the Boston office, I moved to London to open a UK office, we fell in love, married and planned our lives together.

Although we'd both spent two years travelling across the world to visit one another and loved to travel, nothing had prepared us for life in Cambodia. Phnom Penh was dirty, smelly and chaotic. Our home for the first few weeks was a no-frills $10 a night guesthouse. We spent our days trying to learn Khmer (the native language) — a task which made our heads spin due to the language's Sanskrit foundation and absence of a Romanized alphabet. It all felt very unfamiliar and strange. Skip settled in right away and loved the chaotic, dusty, third-world city that was our new home while I felt a bit overwhelmed by it all. My first blog post started like this:

"We've been here less than 24 hours and I'm struggling to find the words to explain how it feels. Dirty roads, wild drivers, lack of any system of traffic control, broken down buildings, stifling heat and a feeling of being so very completely out of my element that I'm not quite sure how to deal with it.

"I'd imagined a sophisticated, worldly city where we could get most of the things we have at home, find nice restaurants and walk through interesting neighbourhoods. Instead, I'm experiencing a place that's nothing of the kind. The streets are chaotic and it's impossible to try and cross a road without lingering on the edge, holding your breath as motorbikes, tuk-tuks, cars, bicycles and street vendors whiz by in a senseless mess of disorder and confusion. The sidewalks are broken up and filled with garbage. Everything stinks. The heat is stifling and I'm constantly damp from head to toe. There are chickens on the street. Nothing is sophisticated. Nothing is cute. It is all incredibly overwhelming, scary and weird."

One year later, here's what I wrote:

"It's no longer stinky. It's aromatic. The broken up sidewalks and chaotic traffic are not an irritation. They're an amusement. Even the searing heat is no longer intolerable. It's a method of bonding with neighbours and friends as we sweat, mop our brows and laugh at one another.

"Within a couple of weeks, I didn't notice the dirt — I saw a tiny, brown-eyed girl playing with a puppy in the sand. Within a month, I didn't recoil at the sight of slabs of bloody meat hanging in the market — I watched street vendors barbecue them and serve them with spicy noodles. And before long, I didn't whine about the stifling heat — I jumped onto the *back of a moto or headed for air-conditioned coffee shops which I did eventually find.*

"I've eaten snake and roasted ants, ridden a four-hour bus journey on a plastic stool and pushed a tuk-tuk up a hill. I've got myself lost jogging through a Muslim village, hiked up Phnom Bakheng at dawn to watch the sun rise over Angkor Wat and learned how to speak a language I'd never even heard of.

"I've dusted bugs from my breakfast cereal, watched a rat run across our living room floor, boiled water for drinking and toasted slices of bread over our gas stove before we broke down and finally bought a toaster.

"I've interviewed indigenous women on remote mining sites for an Oxfam position paper, listened to stories from colleagues whose families were murdered by the Khmer Rouge and helped raise funds for SomOn, our tuk-tuk driver friend, to build his first house.

"I've also eaten freshly shucked oysters and sipped margaritas on the beach as the sun sets over the Gulf of Thailand. I've heard world-class jazz in a Phnom Penh cocktail lounge and savoured cupcakes better than any I've found anywhere in the world. I've awoken to the sounds of the jungle from a room open to the elements in a coastal resort and I've travelled to other parts of Asia on airline tickets costing only a dollar. Far from our original fears of not being able to find anything, we've found everything."

So what changed? We did.

Within the first couple of months, we found a large, comfortable apartment on a quiet tree-lined street and got to know SomOn, our tuk-tuk driver, who became one of our first Cambodian pals. Through him — and our colleagues at work — we made personal connections with local people who taught us more than we'd learn in any book or programme on cultural awareness. We observed how people who had nothing were always willing to give. And we saw how a population that had been persecuted and mistreated was without bitterness and always disposed to laughter.

We met expats from around the world, most of whom had come to Cambodia to give, and our circle of friends included people from Australia, England, the US, the Netherlands, France, Italy and New Zealand. Much of the time we chose to frequent tiny Cambodian hole-in-the-wall cafes and restaurants instead of Western-style establishments and we'd opt to spend time with Tony (our other tuk-tuk driver friend) in his simple one-room, un-air-conditioned home rather than hang out with other expats in upscale residences.

Our work lives took us to places we'd never have seen as a visitor to the country. I worked at an NGO that helps impoverished village people become more self-sufficient so I often found myself in meetings, sitting on grass mats on dirt floors with chickens and pigs snuffling around my feet. Skip worked at an organisation that lobbied the government for financial transparency in the oil, gas and mining revenues coming into Cambodia and soon learned plenty about an industry and a government he'd previously known nothing about.

We'd landed in Cambodia with backgrounds in writing, marketing and business management and soon discovered we were pretty valuable commodities. Work opportunities started coming to us unexpectedly even though we weren't looking for them, and they all opened doors to new circles of friends, new ways of life and new ways of fitting in in this foreign country which quickly became our home.

I'm a research and social media junkie so I spent hours online making contact with people through LinkedIn, as well as joining organisations, attending events and spreading our net so that we brought new people into our lives. I wrote for local online publications and was hired by an NGO to write a book about traditional Cambodian desserts (*The Sweet Tastes of Cambodia*), followed by an assignment writing a book about moving to Cambodia (*The Definitive Guide to Moving to Southeast Asia: Cambodia*). Skip was hired for consulting and marketing projects for Cambodian organisations so we both had ways to supplement our small stipends at the NGOs.

The cost of living is extremely low in Cambodia, so our lifestyle included dinners out most nights of the week and plenty of trips for weekends or longer to other parts of the country and Southeast Asia. But the best parts of living in Cambodia were the people and the simplified way of life. Gone were the stresses of monthly bills (everything is cash) and traffic jams (we got around by tuk-tuk and nowhere was farther than 20 minutes). In their place were gentler, kinder attitudes, open-minded tolerance and acceptance. And after landing in a country I first found to be uncomfortable and strange, Skip and I came to crave — and cherish — the strangeness.

While we missed family and friends, we made trips back home, both to the US and England, and used Skype, Facebook and email to keep in touch. We regularly wrote on our blog (TheMeanderthals.com) and had several visitors from home who came to join us on our adventures. We maintained a US address at Skip's sister's home so we could continue to have a foothold in the States (and a mailing address and address for credit cards) and limited our purchasing of anything that we didn't consider essential (it took almost four months before we bought a toaster as we felt it would tie us down!).

After living in Cambodia three years, we decided to pull up anchor once again so we could find magic in other parts of the world. We spent four months travelling in Asia — a month in India, a month in China, three weeks in Vietnam and three weeks in Thailand (an unplanned excursion due to Skip landing malaria and having to be hospitalised and recuperate in seaside resorts) — then started house sitting (through TrustedHouseSitters.com and MindMyHouse.com).

Since December 2013, we've "lived" in England (twice), France (twice), Cyprus, Italy, Portugal, Nicaragua and Greece. We've taken care of prize-winning Persian cats in Oroklini, had a houseful of rescue animals in Comigne, become best friends with a woolly Golden Retriever in Lewes and hung out with a feral cat in Gialova. It's a wonderful lifestyle and one we've now become quite addicted to.

We do, however, miss Cambodia with its embracing warmth and wonderful people and feel it has spoiled us forever. We no longer care for life in the Western world, with its fast pace, enormity of choice and frequent lack of compassion. We've also learned a lot in the past four years. We've learned we often prefer being around people who don't speak English. We know we'd rather ride on a tuk-tuk or in the back of a bus than drive a car. We've discovered we need very little "stuff" (all we take with us fits into two suitcases and two backpacks). We've realised we'd rather spend time with local people in local restaurants than go to fancy establishments. We've discovered you can understand everyone — no matter what language they speak — with a smile and a photo. We've learned there's magic everywhere and that no matter how much chaos and dirt there may be on the surface, all you have to do is dig to find it.

Frank (Skip) and Gabrielle (Gabi) Yetter
Ages 60 and 55, respectively
From the US & UK, respectively / Always on the move

Gabi and Skip Yetter are both former journalists and published authors who sold their home, quit their jobs and moved to Cambodia in 2010. They are presently travelling around the world house-sitting. They have no plans to go back. Their blog is: www.themeanderthals.com, *and Gabi's writing portfolio is at:* GabrielleYetter.com. *They recently published* Just Go! Leave the Treadmill for a World of Adventure, *available on Amazon.*

"The world is a book and those who do not
travel read only one page."
— St. Augustine

Found in Buenos Aires

Jerry Nelson

The men in the eagle and hawk regalia swooped and swirled around the edges of the circle. In the middle stood the holy man with his vestments. On one side of the circle a warrior entered; from the opposite side, a squaw. Each was accompanied by a small entourage that stood in for missing family and distant ancestors.

Wrapped in blue blankets, the warrior and squaw met in front of the holy man. A sacrifice of tobacco, the repeating of vows and the exchange of hunting knives left just one more ritual. The blue blankets were removed and together they were wrapped in one large blanket. The symbol of two lives becoming one.

I was the warrior and Ale, my wife, was the squaw.

A Virtual Traveling Companion

Even though our wedding was an unusual way to start a marriage, it wasn't the most improbable part of our relationship. How we met and "courted" is the stuff movies are made of.

A friend of Ale's who lived in Nevada came across my blog and website and passed it on. From Buenos Aires, Ale started following the adventure and was with me, through bits and bytes, when I got caught in a buffalo stampede in Washington State and spent six weeks in the Arizona desert with the drug cartels.

We finally met at the Cherokee Powwow in Tennessee when she came to America on vacation. A week later we were married in a traditional Indian wedding ceremony hosted by the Indians on the famous — and infamous — Trail of Tears.

Ale Heads to Buenos Aires; I Head to Washington

Ale and I had talked about where to live after the wedding. We decided I would make a brief visit to Argentina and we'd settle in America. I didn't realize it at that moment, but the instant I said "I do," I was destined to become an expat.

Ale had one week left before she had to return to Buenos Aires and her job as an Executive Secretary for a development firm. I had a month and a half of work in Washington D.C. covering events surrounding President Obama's second inauguration as well as the Veterans' takeover of Veteran's Affairs.

When I snapped the shutter for the final time and filed the last image with the media, it was time to start working through the remaining details before leaving.

I imagine many people have experienced bigger challenges immigrating. Mine was simple. First on the list was to get a new passport to replace the old one with ripped pages from years of adventure photography. I made a trip to a granite and marble bureaucracy in Washington and had the shiny, new passport in 24 hours. Sometimes it helps to be well-known in the nation's capital.

The next morning a friend dropped me off at Dulles International. Hoisting my duffle bag, I shook his hand and was on my way.

"Making it through the day in a country where you live and don't speak the language brings out the need to be creative in simply living life day to day."

The plane lifted off into the sunrise. As it banked sharply to avoid the airspace of the White House, I settled into my seat. With a long flight ahead, I had some time to reflect. Born and raised in Virginia, I was around cameras and travel my whole life. I never thought combining the two would eventually become a career. I also never knew it could take me to the land of the Tango.

My career has been good to me and I've gotten to see things most people see only on television.

As a freelance photojournalist, I had visited and worked in 155 countries by the time the earth made 58 trips around the sun. I was used to the blank stares I would get when trying to order coffee in Japanese, get a hotel room for the night in Russian or get lunch in Riyadh. But I could ask for wifi in 43 different languages. Don't be impressed, "wifi" is the same all over the globe.

It was a long flight with plenty of time to think about what had been my life and wondering what may happen in the days and months ahead. When the plane touched down in Buenos Aires, the wondering stopped.

Within 30 minutes of landing, I pissed off my first Argentine.

Welcome to Argentina

"Mi esposa es muy dulce!"

The customs officer gave me a blank stare. I didn't know if he didn't hear me or my Spanish was that bad. I tried again.

"*Mi esposa es muy dulce!*"

This time he heard me. With the bored expression of a six-year old at Christmas Eve Mass, he nodded and grunted, "Okay. I get that your wife is very sweet... but do you have anything else to declare?"

I shook my head no. In one motion the agent stamped my passport, slid it back across the desk and jerked his thumb toward the door marked *Salida*.

I was in my new home. Welcome to Argentina. It wouldn't be the last time I would be challenged by not knowing Spanish.

Making it through the day in a country where you live and don't speak the language brings out the need to be creative in simply living life day to day.

The Workaround

Many businesses in Buenos Aires have a take-a-number machine near the door. The less progressive businesses are missing the "scoreboard" that shows the "now serving" number.

This created a problem in the beginning. Without the scoreboard, I couldn't tell the difference between B89 and D42.

I quickly learned to take three numbers from the machine. When the clerk would call a number and no one would answer, I'd start paying close attention. If the clerk called a second number, and still no one answered, I knew what was happening and the next number would be mine.

The pharmacy caught on to my trick and posted a sign that I can assume said, "One number only please."

I had to develop another game plan.

If no one was in front of me at the take-a-number machine, I waited until someone pulled a number from the dispenser. Then I'd grab the next ticket and wait for the person in front of me to be helped. I knew I would be next. My tactic hasn't always been convenient, but it's always successful.

Now I am slowly learning to distinguish the last digit and shopping is easier.

Beauty in Belgrano

Ale and I live in the leafy barrio of Belgrano. With a good mix of single-family homes and skyscraper-ish apartment buildings, Belgrano has always been an upper-middle-class neighborhood. Similar to Embassy Row in Washington, there are 16 embassies in the barrio and 13 of them are within four blocks of home.

I didn't pick Belgrano. Ale did. Our apartment is one she bought 15 years ago, and she made a good choice of the apartment and the neighborhood.

To get an idea of Belgrano in 2014, think of Brooklyn in 1964. There are no malls or shopping centers. Big box stores are unheard of and there's not a Walmart around. The stores are very much mom-and-pop and specialized. If you want bread, you go to the baker. If you want meat, you go to the butcher. If you want women's shoes, visit the women's shoe store. You do the same if you're looking for men's shoes. A walk down Avenida Cabildo is a walk back in time.

Every foreign capital has its postcard neighborhood. People who live in the Kodachrome parts of town find it difficult, if not impossible, to experience native life. Here in Buenos Aires, there are three barrios, or neighborhoods, Puerto Madero, Recoleta and San Telmo, that the Argentine version of the Chamber of Commerce puts on their slick, full-color, tri-fold brochures.

Puerto Madero isn't Buenos Aires. It's not even Argentina. It's as if some giant hand scooped up New York City's best parts and plopped them down in the mud along the Rio de Plata. Tourists from Bugtussle, Iowa, come to Buenos Aires, never leave Puerto Madero and then go back home with hundreds of blurry images ready to bore their friends about their time in Argentina. Puerto Madero is no more typical of Argentina than Manhattan is of America.

Recoleta and San Telmo aren't much better. Recoleta is home to the Recoleta Cemetery, the final resting place of Eva "Evita" Peron and other notables. With the chrome, steel and glass high-rises stirred into the chrome, steel, glass and plastic nightclubs, Recoleta is to Argentina as Taco Bell is to Mexican food.

Tourists from Iowa get all breathless when they return home about their visit to the "world's longest yard sale" in San Telmo. It's over a mile long and vendors from all across eastern Argentina show up every Sunday for four hours to mix, mingle, visit and separate the naive from their dollars.

Tourists wander the aisles as they go from stall to stall looking at tchotchkes made in China. Only about one in every 124 booths has genuine Argentine products handmade by the vendor selling them. The visitors from Des Moines hold their plaster tango figurines as proud as any six-year-old kid holding his spelling bee trophy.

As I've traveled, I've always made it a policy to find out where the tourists go and then head in the opposite direction. I've also tried to always keep a little bit of America with me.

Christmas in July

"Christmas in July" is a marketing gimmick in North America. In South America it's reality. Christmas lands in the middle of the Argentine summer. Midnight Mass on Christmas Eve in the Metropolitan Cathedral is a sauna while you get ready to open the gifts. On Christmas 2013 the temperature in the building was 88 degrees. Stir in the body heat of several hundred Argentines and the heat index soared into the low hundreds. The building is 200 years old — and no air-conditioning. Only fans spaced unevenly throughout the building help push the stale body heat around.

In May 2014 as the South American fall started, Ale got tired of hearing my complaints about the weather. My body shouted "winter is coming" but my mind was whispering "baseball season."

She got an inspired idea to calm her "*estupido Americano*."

At her suggestion, we picked a day to celebrate an American Christmas. July 4 falls right in the middle of the coldest weather, so our holiday was set. As Americans enjoyed firecrackers and picnics, we were going to be opening presents, kissing under the mistletoe and listening to Bing Crosby still "Dreaming of a White Christmas" on the stereo.

The last day of June, we started getting ready. Up went the Christmas tree. "Christmas in Dixie" by Alabama filled the apartment. A Charlie Brown Christmas stayed busy on the screen. The only thing missing was *A Christmas Story* and Ralphie's desire for a Red Ryder BB rifle — with a compass in the stock.

Turkey, mashed potatoes, green beans and other memories were laid out. The dining room table was so loaded with food that it was bow-legged and trembling like the fat girl at her first high school dance.

If the turkey was the sun in this galaxy of food, then orbiting just about where Venus would be was a surprise. Blueberries. It's impossible to get cranberries in Argentina. Grown in Chaco province, 100 percent of them are shipped overseas.

Ale did the next best thing. Blueberries.

She went to the corner market, put 100 pesos on the counter and came home with two pints of blueberries. Opening the cookbook made up of recipes from the Hot Springs Presbyterian Women of the Church, she found my mother's recipe, and made "cranberries" for Christmas. If we could substitute Christmas for the Fourth of July, who's to say we couldn't substitute blueberries for cranberries?

That's it for now.

If you ever find yourself in Buenos Aires, Ale and I will — like the man said in the Motel 6 commercial — "leave the light on for you."

Jerry Nelson
US / Buenos Aires

Jerry Nelson is an internationally recognized photojournalist. His work has appeared in a wide variety of publications and news outlets including USA Today, *CNN,* Huffington Post, Upsurge, *CBS,* Dream Row, Earthwalkers *and others. He photographs and licenses images for all manner of commercial and editorial use as well as selling through his website:* JourneyAmerica.org. *You can find him on Twitter at Journey_America.*

"Sometimes I long to forget... It is painful to be conscious of two worlds."
— Eva Hoffman

A Polish Girl Who Had a Dream

Barbara Galewska

My name is Barbara Galewska, I am a Polish woman 31 years old, and I am an expat in Argentina.

I think it all started when I was 13 years old and my parents decided to move to a different city. I had to change schools, friends and routines. I was out of the context I was used to and lost the natural confidence I always had but took for granted. I considered the new place a nightmare, I had no friends and I was bullied at school. I felt lonely like a stranger, like I did not belong, and I hid inside my shell. I began to read hundreds of books, from nonfiction, philosophy and literature to travel books. I was overwhelmed with my own private world and I had a plan for life — to escape from all that was around me. I knew the only way I could make it was to study hard, get enrolled in a good university and be financially and life independent.

So I did. I think I was the only one from my grade who got out of that town after graduating high school. I was accepted to the university 600 kilometers from my hometown. And it was the beginning for me of being happy, self-accomplishing and evolving. I was studying psychology, I made new and great friends, and I felt like I was fulfilling the dream of a sad, frightened teenager. It also felt like this was only the beginning because I wanted more.

While closed in my room, an unhappy teenager discovering new worlds in books, I had this dream and a very deep need for my life to be significant, living in a different way than all the people around me. This need has never fallen asleep. It was always there while making decisions, and I knew my choice must be true to this teenager who never dreamed about a comfortable life but always about an interesting and adventurous life — somewhere far away.

I knew the door to my dreams was to learn languages and I was looking for opportunities to go abroad.

After graduating university I took some small trips and travels for seasonal work. Later I entered a job in the corporate world but knew I was just waiting for my chance. And it finally happened.

I was accepted as a volunteer for a one-year European Union project in Guatemala. With this message the world opened its doors wide for me. It was like a blessing! Without blinking an eye I left my well-paid, prestigious job and the possibilities of building a career in a corporation. I took a flight to one of the economically poorest but culturally richest countries. I became passionate about people, places and cultures. It was going with the flow. I spent nights as a volunteer in a local hospital for malnutritioned babies and days watching people, interacting, developing new passions, tasting all that was new to me and becoming overwhelmed with it. I was also studying hard to learn Spanish because I had said in the job application that I already spoke it.

After one year I went back to Poland as a new person, self-confident and with a unique life experience. I went back to repair my budget and to make a new plan. One of the things I learnt in Guatemala was how to travel cheaply. Again I got a job and after one year of hard corporate work, I was financially ready to go. I took a warm-up trip to Japan. There are some flight bargains in Europe that give you some incredible opportunities to travel without being wealthy. I thought if I could survive by myself on a very low budget for one month in Japan, it would mean I was ready to make this my lifestyle and I could go to Latin America for a year or more. My Japan adventure was an absolute success. After going back home I decided I would buy a ticket to any Latin America country that would be relatively cheap. So I purchased a ticket to Buenos Aires, Argentina. And I haven't been back since!

During my three years here I have travelled from Ushuaia on the southern edge of Argentina to the north of Mexico. I had plenty of jobs such as a photographer in Brazil, a bartender in Peru, a call center operator in Buenos Aires, a tour manager in Colombia and Chile, and a palm tree leaves collector on a Belize island. I've traveled by plane, bus, ferry, boat, tuk-tuk, bike, motorbike and hitchhiking.

My motivation for continuing to travel was always based on this teenage girl's dream but in some ways evaluating and changing it. Basically I wanted to feel like my life had some true meaning, I wanted to feel I was alive. By this I mean learning and trying new things, meeting new people, developing new skills, and coping with new situations, people's differences, and my mistakes and misunderstandings. Whenever I felt I was in danger or a demanding situation, I thought, "If this won't kill me, it will make me stronger," and I felt proud of myself for getting stronger and more experienced.

I was learning about living with local people, how not to be judgmental but respectful and simply positive. I was changing dramatically. I achieved some goals like being independent no matter where, meeting people and feeling extremely comfortable with their companionship, having lots of fun, seeing breathtaking landscapes, and feeling at home without having a home. I was a champion in terms of having incredible, unforgettable romances with men full of passion, beauty and craziness. This all made my heart, my brain and my soul grow and illuminate. I was attracting people with my true laugh, calmness and inside glimmer. I was grateful to the people, to the world, to my fate and my past.

Then came the moment to start sharing this happiness and my passion for life. I had a new dream and it was as strong as this dream from 17 years ago. I dreamed about love. About a true, strong connection based on loving, caring for and respecting each other.

And here I am, sitting on a couch in Rosario, Argentina, eight months pregnant, married to the love of my life, feeling calm, safe, loving and loved. I am a Polish expat in Argentina. I don't know if Argentina is my destination but I know that this term of being an expat is definitely it; and this makes me feel there is nothing like a place I belong to but a state of my mind's freedom.

I am here in my very own context, smiling to a small baby from my future and to all my adventures and experiences from the past. I am sitting on this couch, feeling my baby move inside me, thinking about all the choices I had to make and situations I had to live through to end up here.

A Polish girl who had a dream.

Barbara Galewska
Age 32
Poland / Florianopolis, Brazil

See Barbara's work at: flickr.com/photos/barbaragalewska

Author update: My husband, our son Felipe and I have now moved to Brazil. We settled on a beautiful island and rent a small wooden house surrounded by banana trees, monkeys and beaches. We've made some new friends in our neighbourhood and have started to feel we are in our home-destiny here. I began to work as a psychologist helping Polish people living abroad via Skype. I feel my life is filled with love, gratefulness, joy and some profound meaning.

"Life might be difficult for a while, but I would tough it out because living in a foreign country is one of those things that everyone should try at least once. My understanding was that it completed a person, sanding down the rough provincial edges and transforming you into a citizen of the world."
— David Sadaris

Growing Up in Barcelona

Nia Evans

Where am I? I asked myself repeatedly. As much as the answer seemed to be at the tip of my tongue, I couldn't seem to form a proper sentence. And don't get me wrong, I knew what city I was in, but I found myself unable to understand where I was standing. It was almost like when you see an old painting of some isolated location, such as a chapel or a garden full of poppies, and you sort of feel you know that place. Like maybe you've been there before but you just can't recall. I thought maybe I'd seen that street in a photograph, or in a dream.

But the answer was no clearer than the cloudy gray sky above. "Isn't Barcelona meant to be sunny, mum?" I asked my mother as I skipped over a puddle in my bright orange wellies. I seem to remember her shrugging and telling me that perhaps we'd brought the bad weather along with us.

At the time, I was eight (or eight and three-quarters as I would often announce to anyone who asked), and just a few months prior my mother had made the hasty decision to move abroad. London was becoming increasingly expensive, and for an American who had lived in Europe, settled in England and had a child, taking a few risks now and then wasn't an issue for her at all.

As quickly as the idea had emerged, plans were being made and in what felt like no time (as it does when you're a child), we sat on a stuffy airplane eating fried rice. The flight from London to Barcelona was amusing until an older couple demanded that I pull down my window blind because "the sun is blinding" and "what are you expecting to see out there anyway, a dragon flying alongside us?" After a stern look from my mother and a slight strop, I agreed and started flicking through a scrunched-up duty free magazine.

Before we were able to find an apartment we stayed in nice hotels with free candy, smelly hostels with loud guests, flats in the city center where we could hear passing cars from the bathroom, and finally, a place we could call home. Once we had moved in, our furniture (and more importantly all my toys) that had been shipped to our doorstep arrived in brown boxes that smelled like our old house.

Soon after that my mother started working again and put me in an 'English-speaking' Spanish school. But don't be fooled, it was nothing like anywhere I had been before. First of all, it was a private school about 45 minutes away by car. The uniform consisted of a deep blue skirt, a yellow shirt and a cardigan. Oh, and a tie that I often purposely forgot to wear.

"Spanish kids are strange," I blurted out on my first day when my mother came to pick me up. I remember strongly disliking everything about the school. The playground wasn't like the playgrounds I was used to. It didn't have any trees, and they called it a "patio". The floors were tiled and the boys had strange names like Alejandro, Juan or Sergio. There were some English students, but a vast majority were wealthy Spanish kids whose parents wanted them to learn and have a certain fluency in English.

The older kids were always talking about TV shows, their parents' yachts and summer vacations to expensive places. I didn't like them, and due to the fact I wasn't wearing some top notch shoe brand, I reckon they didn't really like me. I remember thinking that those 'rich kids' were so unaware that they were rich it was hilarious and frightening at the same time.

After a month or so of on-and-off rain, I started to think that the sunny Barcelona scenario was myth, and that it wasn't that much different from London at all. But I liked it, I liked wearing my wellies and my raincoat because I felt protected and warm no matter what the weather. The whole trip had been stressful, as my mother would say, but now that we were settled we could finally start enjoying what the city had to offer. We hopped on those roofless double-decker buses and toured the city, ate salty seafood at poorly lit restaurants, went to noisy festivals where everyone was dancing, and watched Spanish films with English subtitles. And soon enough, the skies cleared and the heat came as summertime approached.

I'd never been a huge fan of the beach, or so I thought. On a hot windy day, my mother and I got the sun lotion, the flip-flops, the huge towels and the stretchy bathing suits and set off for the beach. After a while of ignoring mum's over-enthusiastic attempts to make me get in the water and have fun, I actually decided to do so. And it was fun. The beach was full of children, topless ladies, men with Speedos, and washed-up jellyfish that everyone seemed completely cool about. The sun was hitting the back of my neck as I sat carefully inspecting the shells I had found, and I thought about asking mum whether we could come back tomorrow. At that exact point, I wondered if I'd ever take the beach for granted.

The next day I woke up in agony, sobbing and whining. My mother said we hadn't worn enough sunblock and were burnt from the beach. That was probably the first time ever I had a sunburn like that. It was terrible and stung even in the shower. *I hate the beach,* I thought as I sat in bed looking cross and annoyed.

Throughout the year, the city would sleep and rise again. It would feel calm and then chaotic. Women in long *sevillana* dresses would march proudly down the streets with their chins pointing upwards, and buskers in the metro would strum their guitars even more passionately when they saw the police approach. Trends would come and go like trains at the stations, and the same hits would be played on the radio all day. In the morning the elderly would feed the pigeons at city squares as the young children rushed to school with their heavy backpacks.

Since then, many summers, many seafood dishes, many Spanish classes, many olives (they're in everything), many long walks in flip-flops and many sunburns later, I can actually say I feel Spanish. And in hindsight, it's almost as if things were different back then, as if they've changed drastically since I was a small child.

But I'm guessing I'm the one that's changed the most.

Nia Evans
Age 17
UK / Barcelona, Spain

"Splendid to arrive alone in a foreign country and feel the assault of difference. Here they are all along, busy with living; they don't talk or look like me. The rhythm of their day is entirely different; I am foreign."
— Frances Mayes

The Emotional Rollercoaster That Is Expat Life

Els Mahieu

My name is Els. I was born on a hot April day in a small Belgian village where nothing exciting ever happens. Everyone knows everyone and for a lot of people the next village is considered abroad. I never really felt like I fit in and by the age of 18, I started to think there must be a bigger world out there.

My travels started off on a small scale with city trips to London, Paris and other European cities, but with every trip my curiosity grew stronger. The world out there was beautiful and inspiring and I was determined to see it. I started exploring other continents, much to the despair of my parents who couldn't understand what was so exciting about getting lost in strange cities, eating food that could make you ill and meeting strangers who didn't speak your language. No, travelling was definitely not in the genes of my family!

All this travelling was great, but after a while these two-week trips weren't enough to satisfy my hunger for discoveries! I was longing to stay away longer and get to the bottom of a place instead of just passing through. So after some thinking I decided to help out in different places in the world in exchange for free accommodation and food.

So there I was in March 2010 on a plane to Spain to help out in a small boutique hotel. I had the time of my life and this great experience was soon followed by similar adventures in Albania, Portugal and Northern Ireland. Little did I know that this would change my life completely.

"Being an expat does strange things to you. It's a real eye-opener and makes you look at your home country with totally different eyes. It teaches you a lot about yourself too."

In Northern Ireland I became fond of the person I worked with. I didn't really foresee any future for us, though, knowing how holiday romances usually turn out. But Arnie came to visit me in Belgium, I went back to Northern Ireland and we both became frequent Ryanair flyers. It went on for nearly three years and as romantic and exciting as it was, I wanted more. I had enough of counting the days until we would meet again, of parting after a few days together.

In 2013 I took my car, all my belongings and my lovely English Bulldog Zoé to Belfast. The world was full of new possibilities and I was ready for the next chapter in my life, even if it meant leaving my job, friends and family behind. It wasn't an easy decision: I knew my parents would never be brave enough to jump on a plane, I knew I would see my nephews grow up through Facebook instead of playing with them every week, I knew I would miss the crazy adventures with my friends. But it was something I had to do! The only thing I didn't want to give up was my apartment, so I decided to rent it out. It left me with a security in case I wanted to come back one day.

The first weeks in Belfast were filled with administrative red tape, job hunting and exploring the countryside of Northern Ireland. The red tape was frustrating and I found out there is no such thing as a European Union when it comes to rules and regulations. After a month, I was lucky enough to find a job. I enrolled in a few meet-up groups to socialize and was lucky enough to work with a lot of other expats, so meeting people was never a problem. Yes, my new life here was going great! What an adventurer I was, right?

Wrong. I went back to Belgium for a few days, saw my family and friends, ate the food I was used to eating all my life, enjoyed the sunnier climate — and for the first time in my life I thought: this is my country, this is where I belong.

When I came back to Ireland, I started to see everything in the negative: I didn't like the fatty food, the people had no fashion sense whatsoever, it was grey all the time and it was just plain old boring! I forced myself to see the good sides: people are friendly and polite, the landscapes are absolutely stunning and

Belfast is a city in full expansion. But every time I saw something on the news about Belgium, I secretly wished I was there.

What was happening to me? Wasn't I the world traveller who could live anywhere? Wasn't I the person who always claimed, "The world is my home"?

I knew that if I wanted this to work, I would have to stop seeing everything so negatively, I would have to stop comparing with my old life in Belgium and focus on the good sides and the chances I was given to discover a new country! So I tried to pull myself together.

Where am I now? I guess somewhere in between. When Belgium did well in the World Cup, I was really proud of my country and wished I was there to celebrate with my friends. But when Scotland wanted to vote for independence, I felt closely related because I didn't want the United Kingdom to split up. I even work for the Belfast tourist office now! I welcome travellers and visitors to my city, explain to them what they can see or do here and give them tips about restaurants and pubs. This is probably the best proof that I managed to turn the dark pages! I guess it's safe to say I have a much healthier approach to living here than I did back then.

Being an expat does strange things to you. It's a real eye-opener and makes you look at your home country with totally different eyes. It teaches you a lot about yourself too. I am glad I made the decision to move abroad and although the general culture here might not be my kind of thing, I know now that I am capable of leaving everything behind to start a new life somewhere else.

Lately I am more and more attracted to the Spanish lifestyle. I know the pitfalls and I know that if I decide to go, it will not be easy. But I might just be willing to give it a try!

Note: When I feel homesick, I listen to the same nostalgic song about my home country: "Le Plat Pays" from Jacques Brel. You can listen to it and see the English lyrics here: lyricstranslate.com/en/le-plat-pays-flat-land.html.

Els Mahieu
Age 39
Belgium / Northern Ireland

Els is originally from Belgium, living the expat life in Northern Ireland. As an avid traveller, Els loves to meet locals and can never resist the temptation of a local food market! Culture, food and slow travel make her tick. Follow her adventures on myfeetaremeanttoroam.com.

"You will never be completely at home again, because part of your heart always will be elsewhere. That is the price you pay for the richness of loving and knowing people in more than one place."
— Miriam Adeney

Discovery

Rebecca Conklin

"Things arise and she lets them come, things disappear
and she lets them go." — Tao Te Ching

I hadn't brushed my hair in a week. My teddy-bear T-shirt fell below orange neon spandex shorts. In that second-grade florescence, I didn't care that I appeared feral and pantsless. I probably didn't even notice, hard at work on my map of Central and South America. Exploring coastlines, coloring borders, circling capitals.

How did I understand it then, the earth and all its people? To me, the world outside my wooded cul-de-sac was nothing more than faces on TV and my grandparents who lived in The Mountains. In a How Many Marbles in the Jar? contest, to which the correct answer was over 500, I had guessed 52. I was still confused if root beer was beer or soda and so refused to drink it. Every day as an eight-year-old was a journey through the incomprehensible.

And despite great odds, in that second-grade class-room, staring at the 8.5 by 11 frame meant to teach me of the world, I made my greatest discovery. In the isthmus between Central and South America, I saw a crack. A sliver of water so small my blunt blue crayon couldn't stay in the lines. It hit me like a dodge ball: these pieces of land were not connected. My hand shot up in the air. *Call the papers*, I thought. I could read the headline already.

My teacher came and I showed her, beaming. She smiled and turned to the class.

"Rebecca's found the Panama Canal. Who knows what that is?"

The what? I thought. Before I could explain my discovery, Sally Somebody raised her stupid hand and told us with her stupid voice about digging and boats going from the Pacific to the Atlantic.

I'd been sabotaged by my brain, by not understanding that a slice of water on a map was not a discovery because it was drawn by someone who had already seen it, or at least heard about it from the millions of other people who had already seen it.

And this is what it is to move abroad: feral and pantsless, without the slightest clue of what's going on in the world around you, obliviously certain you are an explorer on the path to discovery. And then Sally Somebody ruins it by proving that there's nothing in the world that hasn't been discovered. And you're still confused about root beer.

I moved to Shanghai just three months after graduating college to teach at an international high school. I'd gone to a tiny school in the mountains of North Carolina whose enrollment barely rivaled the town's population of 800. And yet when I landed in Shanghai, a megapolis with a population of over 24 million, I wasn't overwhelmed. In the van from the airport, I looked at people riding bikes and endless towers and everything felt just as it should.

There are plenty of moments in planning to move abroad that overwhelm. Imagining yourself in a sea of strangers, as if by Google map, on the other side of the world. Wondering how you will possibly communicate or find your way. Finding friends or, my biggest concern at the time, an IKEA and a foreign-language bookstore. It's the anticipation, not the act, that makes it a great feat. As if you're Odysseus leaving Ithaca or the Little Prince leaving asteroid B-612. But all you actually have to do is board a plane like you're headed to Minneapolis. It really is that simple.

From there, each moment transitions easily into the next and everything seems just as it should. Yes, that man just spoke to me in Chinese. Yes, this car is driving in the middle of three lanes. Yes, here that is possible. Yes, I'll eat steamed buns and warm soymilk for breakfast. And it continues to move in roughly the same way for however long you decide to stay. Perhaps that's why I'm still here, six years later.

Saying yes in variations of enthusiasm may be another reason why I'm still here. I made a two-part promise to myself on the plane to Shanghai:

- I would (try) to let go of expectations.
- I would say yes as often as possible (or safe/ reasonable).

Start practicing these wherever you are and your life will come alive. These are, I've found, the essential survival skills for those who embark on expat life, which can be as isolating, alienating and lonely as it is fulfilling, life-affirming and transformative. With these two principles in mind, I naively navigated Shanghai, made friends, furnished my apartment in Scandinavian simplicity and finally curled up with a good book in a language I could read.

> *"In my wanderings, I've heard many talk about one of the pleasurable anxieties of travel: entrusting others. You become vulnerable to the hospitalities and promises of complete strangers. And when you make it through, you arrive home with a slightly stronger faith in humanity, in our ability to uphold the promise of another's trust."*

And it was these two principles that got me out of my comfort zone (of couches, cafes, and books) to race fixed gear bikes in lawless traffic, eat fried scorpion and eel testicle, manage my own and others' crises (the worst was a friend's drunken impalement by glass, perhaps after one too many yeses at the Qingdao Beer Festival), and follow a lone monk into a dark cave on Christmas (it seemed reasonable at the time and, as it turned out, he was a perfectly fine monk).

In ancient Chinese Daoist philosophy, a foundational concept is wu wei. Do without doing. It's basically a go-with-the-flow kind of idea, but to an extreme that may make continental philosophers uneasy. As you as strive to achieve, your aim escapes you. As you try to gain control, you lose control. It's a philosophy of paradox that highlights the require-ments of truly living.

In the repetition of our "normal" lives, it is easy to fall into routines that pull us to say no more often than we say yes. It is easy to wrap our lives around complex and often unspoken expectations rather than being thankful and accepting of how life presents itself. But this isn't wu wei. It isn't the way to live a life with graceful vulnerability.

Accepting life abroad without going crazy is accept-ing wu wei. It's not trying to make a discovery that no one else has made, or getting to more countries than anyone else you know, or finally mastering a foreign language. It's letting go of expectation, remembering to say yes and offering yourself to the flow.

If there is one thing that, I believe, binds the diverse group that makes up any international community abroad it's that, whether they call it such, they have accepted and embodied wu wei in the core of their being. I imagine living abroad with strict expecta-tions and routines would be exhausting and incredibly unfulfilling. It's wu wei that opens us to the experi-ence. When we are open to experience, experience is also open to us.

And as for discovery vis-à-vis my second-grade desk-bound explorer, it turns out it's pretty simple. In a world that has already been discovered by all of the people who have lived in it long before me, the only thing left to discover is myself. It's the only place no one else has been and no one else will ever go.

In my wanderings, I've heard many talk about one of the pleasurable anxieties of travel: entrusting others. You become vulnerable to the hospitalities and promises of complete strangers. And when you make it through, you arrive home with a slightly stronger faith in humanity, in our ability to uphold the promise of another's trust.

Something similar happens when you live abroad. You become vulnerable to yourself. Without familiar friends, important plans, and fancy possessions, you connect with a self that isn't fully settled. A self that is still figuring some things out. And when you make it through, you arrive home (probably a very different place now than when you started) with a stronger faith in yourself, in your ability to uphold the promise of your own potential. And that may be the single biggest discovery you can ever hope to make.

Rebecca Conklin
Age 29
US / Shanghai / US

Rebecca Conklin is a graduate student in Composition and Communication at Central Michigan University. She spent her 20s traipsing Asia with a home base in Shanghai. She recently moved back to the states for love, the only thing more essential than life abroad.

Moving to Medellín

Lisa Imogen Eldridge

If anyone had ever told me I would be living in Colombia, I would have laughed.

I knew little of the country, except where it was in the world and what it had once been famous for. I had no expectations and at the time I thought I would be just passing through as I looked for somewhere to settle in Latin America.

"You're going where?" people would ask, surprised at my choice of relocating to the other side of the world. Knowing that I could have a better quality of life than in England, I knew Latin America would offer me everything I was looking for: salsa dancing, a great climate and most importantly a way out of the nine-to-five rat race I no longer wanted to be part of. So I left on a one-way ticket, unsure where or even if I would find a place I wanted to call home.

But as the plane flew into Colombia, I felt an overwhelming feeling of complete certainty that this was where I needed to be.

Once the most dangerous city in the world, Medellín is now one of the biggest success stories. Just over a decade ago, parents were afraid to send their children to school in case they never saw them again. Forward to 2013 and Colombia's second largest city was awarded the Most Innovative City Award, beating Tel Aviv and even New York.

"But the real reason this city has completely blown me away is the energy. The energy of the mountains surrounding the valley and the energy of the people."

So why do I love living in Medellín?

It's not called the city of eternal spring for nothing and being a pleasant 27 degrees Celsius year-round is definitely a bonus. Yes, it rains and there are storms but because the city's in a valley, the storms are simply amazing to watch, especially from an apartment with a view.

The views here are astounding and each morning I feel lucky to be able to stare out at the mountains and the city skyline in the distance. I have been to 100 countries and the views here never fail to astonish me, especially at night when the city comes alive.

Like many other Brits, I have a love of football and so do the Colombians. Being here for the World Cup and supporting both England and Colombia was the best experience I could have asked for. Football games are shown constantly across the city from shopping malls to bars and restaurants, and I love that I can get the Premiership here too. I just need to find a man who doesn't mind me watching the footie as we dine.

A night out here is much cheaper than in the UK and I've adapted to the *paisa* culture — a bottle of aguardiente which you simply drink in shots throughout the evening. One of my passions is dancing and Colombians love to dance, whether it's salsa, bachata or reggaeton. They even have my favourite music — electronic — which I can find in selected clubs. Taxis are economical too and they are everywhere, so it's easy to get around. Not being able to afford taxis in the UK, I regularly take them here.

Price is one of the biggest factors and I even lived in a penthouse for two months, something I never thought I would be able to do. After living in a box room in London for double the price, I can see why this city is attracting so many people looking for a better quality of life.

But the real reason this city has completely blown me away is the energy. The energy of the mountains surrounding the valley and the energy of the people. I realise there is a real sense of pride for people living here and it's contagious. Locals say hello and the security guards are beyond friendly. Policemen wave as they pass in their trucks and there's hardly any litter to be seen. Residents are made to feel part of the city with renovation projects such as the cable car and outdoor escalators that serve as public transport for those who live in the poorer pueblos on the mountains.

Medellín has come far in the last decade and I am proud to say that I live in this city, a city of people who look only to the future.

I came to Latin America with the hope that I would find a home, and I didn't get farther than the first country I landed in. They say that home is where the heart is, and Medellín definitely has my heart. Even if there are days when I find myself dreaming of marmite on toast and a traditional cup of English tea, I know that I am where I am meant to be.

Lisa Imogen Eldridge
Age 39
England / Colombia

Lisa Imogen Eldridge has travelled extensively as a solo traveller and has now visited 100 countries. Lisa's mission is to empower women with her website, girlabouttheglobe.com, *a resource for women travelling solo.*

It's Easy to Fall in Love with Life in Thailand!

Laura Gibbs

For countless years Thailand has topped the polls for best place to go on holiday. With stunning natural scenery, white sandy beaches, amazing food and friendly locals, who doesn't want to visit? Compared to America or Europe, Thailand is cheap — meaning you get low-cost luxury on your holiday. Thailand also tops the polls when it comes to best places to live as an expat, but frequently people who come on holiday to scope out Thailand as a potential retirement destination miss the key factors of what it really means to be an expat here.

On holiday you aim to relax, explore, treat yourself and 'see' Thailand (temples, islands, shopping malls, great sites), yet if you come on holiday you are one step removed and quintessentially still at home. There is a duality to your mindset and you are aware that it's temporary. You compare it to home all the time and most likely you will see the best of Thailand but also the worst. "Oh, the food is too spicy", "people are so poor", "there is too much traffic", "it's so nice but I couldn't afford to live like this all the time", "the sex industry is awful". Thais also notice this duality in holidaymakers and often ask, "Where you from, country?" in an attempt to understand foreigners better.

Some people are unlucky and they manage to hit the tourist trail. They see all the must-see spots of Thailand but are constantly surrounded by other tourists and Thai 'tour guides' who are experts in making you spend a few extra dollars. The best example is at the Royal Palace in Bangkok — 'tour guides' often tell you it's closed that day and then suggest a city tour with them. Many people fall for this but it's not terrible. You end up with a nice tour of the Big Mango and you aren't even aware the 'tour guides' have conned you. Everyone's happy.

Being an expat in Thailand is totally different than being on holiday here. It's crazy, it's silly and at times it's aggravating, but more than any of these, it makes you feel alive! Living in the kingdom of smiles allows you to wash your worries away and soak up the good vibrations.

In the last 10 years Thailand has made itself open to what they class as long-stay tourists and what we would call expats. There are three main reasons the Kingdom attracts so many expats and long-stay tourists.

Quality of life for expats

The combination of value for money and low costs makes Thailand an expat haven. It's a country where an average meal for two with drinks will set you back around $10 or a street stall dish just $1, and a studio apartment costs less than $200 monthly including utilities. Combine this with cheap flights to Bangkok from just about anywhere and you have a great place to live. Suddenly money is no longer an issue as (outside of Bangkok) you can afford just about everything. The cheap meals and studio apartment will be delicious and comfortable — you will not be roughing it. Thailand allows you to live the way you wanted if money weren't an issue, and this is the best gift an expat can have.

Weather and nature

Good weather matters more to personal happiness than most people realise. If the sky is constantly grey or if you are feeling the cold, then you can never fully unwind. Imagine the feeling of the first real spring day — the sun beaming down, the grass a vibrant green and the sky a bright, cloudless blue — your mood immediately lifts. Now imagine that you could see that sky and the sun all the time. That's why there are so many Europeans in Thailand.

But more than the weather, Thailand is brimming full of nature. The north is full of condensed tropical jungle with elephants and mountains. The south boasts long, sandy white beaches, tropical islands with bamboo huts and fruit smoothies whilst the capital, Bangkok, offers modern amenities, a shopper's paradise and anything you might possibly miss from home!

Ease of living in Thailand

It's natural to want to be off the beaten track (in deepest Botswana) or to experience a culture fully different from your own (Japan, for example) but many expats forget that those experiences come with some degree of hardship — language difficulties, an unusual cuisine that can lead to Delhi belly, basic accommodation and standard of living, boredom, culture shock, etc.

Thailand is somewhat different. Because there are so many tourists visiting every year and because many of them end up becoming expats, all your creature comforts are available. From international supermarkets to Western style apartments and restaurants offering food from every country around the world; if you miss it, chances are you can find it. Thailand isn't over-run with expats, but Thais are so used to catering to the wants of tourists that the attempts to please foreigners naturally spills over to the expats. And because the country is so geared to deal with tourists, local travel is easy and most Thais speak basic English (although they go crazy over foreigners who can speak a little Thai)!

It's hard not to fall in love with Thailand. As well as the above reasons, there are hundreds of other personal reasons making the Kingdom the top expat destination. Seeing a Thai smile is almost reason enough — a friendly curious smile at the foreigner, an apologetic smile when one driver is in the wrong, a genuine smile when you purchase something at the market or that smile of satisfaction from a chef when they see you are enjoying their meal.

Foreigners are welcomed even by other expats. The sense of expat community is strong in Thailand, with countless expats willing to offer advice and recommendations to newbies. Making the move is also very easy if you allow it to be. Apply for a triple entry tourist visa or (if you are over 50) a retirement visa, pack a suitcase and some sunscreen, book a ticket and go. You don't need to plan ahead in Thailand. Once you are here you will find what you need. Accommodations? Ask around and you will find them, no need for a year-long contract, mortgage or hefty security deposit. Friends? Talk to the person at the next table; I promise they will respond with a smile. Sunshine and nature? Right on your doorstep.

So what is the difference between tourists and expatriates in Thailand? Tourists come to be wowed by the country, expats are wowed by the people. Tourists enjoy two weeks of luxury, expats enjoy a comfortable standard of living at a fraction of the cost of home. Tourists take some beautiful pictures, expats see those images every day. Tourists come to relax, expats come to enjoy the most life can offer them!

Laura Gibbs
Age 27
Bristol, England / Thailand

Laura is author of Becoming an Expat: Thailand, *a comprehensive guide including everything you need to know before moving to Thailand (from the city life and dating, to cultural secrets, what to avoid and the best beaches).*

"Peace in my heart
Peace in my soul
Wherever I'm going
I'm already home."
— Betsy Blondin

Cultural Reciprocity and the True Meaning of "Home"

Jessica Beder

What are you running away from? That's what people keep asking me. As though the idea of moving to a foreign country is so absurd that something terrible must have driven me to it.

Following two and a half years in Australia, four months in Guatemala and now a semi-permanent move to Buenos Aires, I am no stranger to the expat lifestyle.

"But your family and friends are here. This is where you grew up. This is your home," they say. What they don't understand is that to me "home" means something different.

In the United States, post-collegiate normalcy is defined by a few simple questions. Where do you live? What do you do? Who do you do it with? For most of us, growing up means settling down and staying put.

I can hear Crosby, Stills, Nash & Young crooning out "Our House" as I picture the picket fence, Volvo and yard full of cats.

According to a trends report compiled by the Pew Research Center, 37 percent of Americans have never left their hometown and 80 percent grow up to live within 20 miles of it.

This strong cultural bond with "home" is why those we leave behind have such a hard time understanding the expat life. American culture is an egocentric vacuum that you don't see clearly until you're outside. Expats take on the perspectives of others around the globe and with each new vista, ideas of life, relationships and the world change.

As months and years tick by, the tapestry of meaning formed from experiential awareness begins to polarize your sense of identity. Suddenly home is not just the place you live. Home is the piece of your soul that finds its counterpoint in the intoxication of cultural reciprocity.

As travelers caught in a matrix of encounters, poetic solitude and adrenalin-pumping exploits, we find ourselves in an ocean of uncharted potential. Not just potential for what we can accomplish as individuals, but for how awareness can help bridge the gaps in global society. Learning about foreign cultures is both my greatest challenge and greatest adventure.

It's not what I am running from but what I am running toward.

How to make the leap
Sometimes I think I should be a spokesperson for Nike because I end up where I do because I "just do it."

Many expats will tell you they spent months or years planning their continental leap, researching every detail and comparing one city to another. That doesn't work for me. If I plan too much, I get totally overwhelmed. Before long I've completely lost my ambition in a cloud of risk analysis and apprehensive confusion.

Before moving to Australia, I knew very little about the country except that 80 percent of the continent's indigenous plants, animals and reptiles are found nowhere else on earth. Naturally, exotic, deadly animals were a big part of the draw. Never mind that any Australian will slap you in the face if you ask what it's like to ride a kangaroo.

The University of Sydney has a degree program that aligned with my career ambitions but aside from that, there was no grand romantic strategy. I just followed my heart.

We can't always find the time or money to make our expat dreams come true. But if it's possible, take the plunge! Life's too short to get hung up on maybes and what-ifs. The world is a cultural buffet and if you don't take a chance, you'll miss out on the richest delights.

While research and preparation can be helpful, too many preconceived ideas may color your impressions. Don't limit your options based on stereotypes or horror stories. It's surprising how often these stories are inaccurate. I don't mean to downplay the need for caution everywhere but these stories should never define your judgment.

It's a beautiful experience getting to know the personality of a land and culture first-hand — the good, the bad and the socially awkward. No matter what people say, it's never quite what you expect. So be bold.

Bold moves

When I bought my one-way ticket to Argentina, I was living in Guatemala and waiting to hear back from a major job opportunity in the US. I had been through two rounds of interviews and it was down to me and one other person.

My work contract came to an end, still with no answer, and I had to decide; do I fly home to the cats and picket fences of Connecticut and wait there, or choose another path? All I knew about Buenos Aires was that it was called "the Paris of South America," but the city had always called to me. I had no idea what to expect but I knew it would be the most inspiring challenge to find out. Without thinking twice, I booked the flight to Buenos Aires, packed, found a home for the kitten I'd accidentally adopted and left Guatemala.

In what I've come to see as a stroke of luck, they chose the other candidate, and here I am still in love with Argentina and my life. If I hadn't seized the moment, I might never have come.

Challenges of the expatriate life

Stepping outside my comfort zone has become a way of life for me because without even realizing it, expats take risks and defy normality at every turn.

Most of us don't fit in. Many of us struggle to find a job. A few of us unintentionally offend everyone we meet. The key is to enjoy it because the challenge of adapting to foreign customs and standards is personal growth at its best.

By far the biggest expat challenge I've experienced was Buenos Aires' not-so-charming culture of stealing. Within three days of arriving, I was freed of two iPhones, my wallet and a Mac computer charger — all on separate occasions, and all lifted straight out of my bag.

People had warned me, but somehow I still wasn't prepared. The best advice I can give to someone in my place is *relax*, and remember that these things happen to everyone now and then. Deal with things one step at a time and don't blame the city.

For me, everything turned out fine and I learned a valuable lesson (finally). Having just come from Guatemala where 70 percent of the population lives below the poverty line, I could hardly lose my head over a silly inconvenience.

Attitude and perspective is everything so if you keep a positive mindset, things will be resolved faster and easier. There's no greater lesson than failure so may yesterday's floor cookies bake me a brighter tomorrow!

Finding work

How do you find a job abroad?

It largely depends on the language, visa requirements and your line of work rather than your qualifications.

In Australia, New Zealand and several other countries, you can get something called a work and holiday visa that allows you the right to work for a year. It's an excellent way to travel while earning money and it buys you time to go on interviews for a permanent position if that's your goal.

Trying to get sponsored permanently can be a soul-destroying process. Unless you are the only qualified applicant (unlikely) or you have a special arrangement with your home country, companies will choose a local candidate over you. I went on hundreds of interviews in Sydney, only to be rejected over and over. It had a devastating impact on my professional self-worth that lasted for years. In the end it was networking, not applications, that got me an offer.

In countries like Argentina where the language barrier can be a huge setback to finding work, things have gone a little differently. While working to establish my freelance writing business, I picked up nanny jobs; and looking for advice and a change of course, I posted on the Buenos Aires Expat Hub, an informational support network for struggling migrants.

Within five minutes of asking the "hubsters" (a collective group of keen-as-a-bean expats, ages 18–75) for tips on finding an English-speaking publishing job, I had three offers to chat and two formal interviews. Six months later, I am happily working my dream job for a company that values my talents, encourages my Spanish and inspires me every day.

Making friends

Making friends is one of the greatest challenges I've faced. My strategy is to move in with local residents. When you first arrive in a new city, it can be completely overwhelming. Where do you buy food, where are the safe ATMs and what busses will take you where you want to go?

Living alone has its perks. However, as an expat there is nothing better than having friendly housemates who are already knowledgeable and can offer advice or new expats eager to learn it all with you. Finding a place to live can be one of the scariest realities of moving abroad but every city has websites dedicated to helping internationals find housing. It's just a matter of finding a sunny café and spending a few hours researching your options.

One caution is to discuss rent prices with a trusted local to make sure you're not being overcharged; it's hard to understand a foreign exchange rate well enough to know what's fair, and people are quick to take advantage. I learned this the hard way.

Outside of housemates, I have a reputation for making friends in odd places. I'll go to the bathroom and come out arm in arm with a girl I never met before — usually because I've embarrassed myself in some way and we've shared a good laugh at my expense. This talent serves me well in foreign cultures.

The trick is to launch into your new home with the energy of an over-caffeinated Labrador. Join Meetup. com to find local events, scout social groups on couchsurfing.com, or just get out of the house and talk to people! It will go better than you think.

Learn the language

You don't need to speak the language of a city to survive in it. I proved that backward and forward visiting Moscow during the Russian winter. But you're missing a vital link to understanding the culture if you don't at least try. While being scammed in Beijing, the con artist taught me to say "I love you" (wall-eye-knee) in Mandarin. I see it as an even trade. Inter-lingual communication unlocks chambers of your brain you didn't know existed.

When I left the US in July 2014, the only thing I knew how to say in Spanish was *el pato no es tuyo* — the duck is not yours. This phrase caused a lot of confusion for the poor Guatemalans who had to deal with my bizarre sense of humor.

Since then, I have taken classes, studied hard and improved a lot. Working in an Argentine office forces me to write emails and give presentations, so the fun never ends. By learning slang words and witty catch phrases, I'm able to chum around with my coworkers in comical disgrace.

In Buenos Aires there are endless opportunities to practice. Three nights a week there is an event called *Intercambia*, where locals and internationals of all cultures have drinks together and practice speaking. It's free and when you arrive, you put little flag stickers on your shirt to indicate what languages you speak. I choose flags for Argentina, the US, and maybe France if I feel like royally embarrassing myself.

Once you have the language basics down, it's a blast to burst out of your comfort zone and approach people. Locals love it when you make an effort, even if your grammar's not perfect — or in my case, remotely intelligible.

There's nothing like language challenges for producing moments of awkward hilarity. As I've discovered, the key is to have no shame. Embarrassing yourself and inadvertently offending everyone around you is a commonplace occurrence in the expat lifestyle, so why not embrace it?

Once I was waiting for a train next to a kind old lady. On my way to the beach for the first time, I was excited and... well, she noticed. Smiling, she asked me where I was going and *way* too pleased with myself, I explained. Unfortunately, I accidentally used the verb that in Argentina, refers to being sexually aroused. Her eyebrows practically launched off her face in surprise.

Probably my worst linguistic disaster was when I confused the conjugation of the verb *tener* (to have). As I descended into the dank subway air, my gaze met with a disheveled homeless man's.

He pierced me with an imploring look. I had no change, so I quickly muttered, "Lo siento, no tienes cambia." (meaning to say *I have no change*).

To my horror, his expression flashed to anger. "Que?" He demanded, "*Que!?*" (*What!?*)" So I repeated over and over, "No tienes cambia! No tienes cambia!" His face was purple with rage. How did he not understand?

I was sad when I realized my mistake a few minutes later. Instead of apologizing, I had been shouting in a homeless man's face, "You have no money, you have no money!"

Another language calamity occurred on a day that I trekked to the local pharmacy in search of medication for a nasty gastro-intestinal virus. At that time my Spanish was okay with general topics like where someone is from or the weather, but with medical or anatomy words, I was lost. Let's just say that describing my intestinal symptoms was my worst turn ever at charades!

Saying goodbye

Unfortunately, one of the hardest parts of the expat life is saying goodbye.

For many of us, there are countless friends and family back home that we work hard to keep strong bonds with. However, while homesickness is not uncommon, it's not the worst kind of parting for expats.

I am referring to the titanic farewells that shatter your identity — the partings that make you question all the decisions you've ever made.

"Crouching beside my fourteen-year-old dog, her milky eyes teemed with liquid trust. Steeling me with her caramel gaze, she took no notice of the suitcase by the door. I cradled her silver muzzle between sweaty palms, trying to strike a balance between denial and an overwhelming appreciation for all that she is." – Journal, March 2012

Travel-hungry expats understand this raw reality better than anyone as we find ourselves meeting and parting from, perhaps forever, a parade of exceptional people.

But what do you do when they become an integral part of your life? How many memories and midnight secrets, how many hugs and happy days do you share before it happens — before they are part of you forever?

Leaving Australia after two and a half years was one of the hardest things I've ever done. Parting from not only a city full of dear friends, but also a culture and a country I love more than anything.

As I have learned, for the true expat there's no such thing as goodbye. Once you have communed with a foreign culture for a substantial length of time, it seeps into your core and becomes a part of who you are.

Addicted to the otherness

The day I arrived in Australia I opened my suitcase to find a small pink envelope tucked into one of my shoes.

Inside was a card that pictured four little girls in tutus stretching on a balance beam — three of them were doing graceful pliés, while the fourth was holding onto the beam upside down like a monkey, tutu and curls everywhere.

"Happy Valentine's Day to a girl who does things differently. I'm so proud of you, love Mom."

That was the first time I realized how unusual my lifestyle is. Since then, I have grown a deep appreciation for my horse-of-a-different-color perspective and the sense of "otherness" I feel from both my host community and my US roots. This may be the best thing about expat life.

Depending on where you've settled and how starkly you stand out from the crowd, people will inevitably pick you out as foreign and the questions will begin.

Much to my amusement, listing ordinary details of my hometown generally sparks a ravenous fascination in the inquirer. "How close are you to New York? What is winter like? Squirrels!" Just like that, the most mundane details of my life become exotic and precious.

And the same phenomenon occurs when you describe your expat life to those back home. This is because explaining a foreign country to someone who's never traveled there is like teaching a blind man to paint. He can hold the brush and imagine the colors, but the artwork can never be actualized to intent.

This is what makes the expat life so great. The inspiration that comes from investing in a foreign culture fills gaps in your soul that you never knew existed.

For me and many expats, "home" is not a place you can travel to — it's a sense of self.

Jessica Beder
Age 29
Connecticut, US / Buenos Aires

Jessica is a writer, scholar and sporadic pragmatist. She believes that curiosity is the key to most things in life, and humor can solve the rest. Currently she lives in Buenos Aires and works as the Content Manager for Nearpod, a revolutionary ed-tech platform. Her blog is Paint by Pursuit.

Living the Good Life in Panama

Terry Coles

After serving for 30 years as a firefighter and paramedic in Corpus Christi, Texas, my husband Clyde decided it was time to call it quits. Although he loved his job, he always felt he had no business running into a burning building as an old man. He had always dreamed of retiring at age 57 but with the high cost of health care in the US and an ex-wife getting a large chunk of his pension, how could we afford to retire?

Then one day he stumbled upon an article about baby boomers retiring abroad in order to live cheaper and he cautiously approached me with the idea. "If we can find a place to live comfortably on my pension, are you willing to retire now?" he asked. I was only 50 years old and I thought, "Do I want to work another 15 years or quit now and enjoy life?" After some serious contemplation I said, "Where are we going and when?"

Neither of us had traveled out of the US other than to the border towns of Mexico. I'd been to Canada a few times but that barely counted as travel abroad. So we buried our faces into some heavy-duty online research wondering where we could go and if we could really make it work.

The countries in Latin America seemed to pop out as having a lower cost of living and many offered good health care. We looked into Belize, Costa Rica, Ecuador, Colombia and Panama to name a few. Although there were positive and negatives about each country, Panama seemed to stand out among the rest.

Boasting that it offers one of the best retirement programs in the world, Panama offers top-notch health care, a warm tropical climate, close proximity to the US and much more. We took action and applied for passports and then planned our first exploratory trip to Panama in 2010.

With a few months of self-taught Spanish under our belts, we landed in Panama excited, naïve and ready to explore the country. My fearless husband pretended he was driving a fire truck as he aggressively nudged his way through gridlocked traffic in Panama City. I remember being shocked by the tenements alongside the highway with curtains flapping in the breeze and clothes drying on the balconies. The stark reality of this poverty provided a backdrop to the cityscape of skyscrapers that lined the horizon. My inner self wanted to run and hide, worrying that this poverty level was our future. Would we have to give up all the comforts we'd come to know if we wanted to retire early and move here?

As we crossed over the Bridge Of The Americas into what they call the interior of the country, the landscape changed. The tall buildings gave way to small cement homes with hammocks in the front yard. The rolling hills were covered with green, lush vegetation that appeared like broccoli florets in the distance. Unusually skinny cows roamed in the pasture below while local men rode by on horseback wearing straw hats. Tiny side roads seemed to climb up into the majestic mountains and reach high into the sky filled with puffy white clouds.

We drove from one end of the country to the other exploring every dirt road along the way. Our rental car made its way up steep mountains and down deserted roads as we accumulated over 1,200 exploration miles on the car. Our hectic lives were behind us now as we entered a world of tranquility where everyone and everything moved in slow motion.

Despite our lack of Spanish, we found the locals to be warm, welcoming and always trying to help. We ate meals for $3 to $4 in local restaurants called fondas and stayed at decent hotels for $50-$60 a night. Having lived in south Texas we welcomed the humid, tropical climate that seemed to embrace us in its warmth. As the days of our vacation passed, we began to realize that this could be a reality if we dared to take the plunge. And since we were looking at retiring at ages 51 and 57, we certainly weren't ready to sit in rocking chairs and get old. Instead, moving abroad could offer us a lifetime of memories, adventures, challenges, new friends and new experiences.

Our last year in Texas was a whirlwind of packing, paperwork and pouting about leaving our kids and friends behind. Clyde worked on paperwork for our visa by sending off documents to be authenticated at our local Panamanian Embassy. Being a self-proclaimed Internet geek, he connected with every Panama expat board to make friends and get information.

One day a Panamanian woman posted an ad about a house for rent in Capira, Panama. It was a three-bedroom, two-bathroom house for just $300 a month. Included were pictures of the lovely home that was just three years old at the time. Clyde called me over to look at the photos and said, "I thought we'd be able to find a house in Panama for this price but certainly not one this nice." Immediately Clyde wrote to the owner and developed a friendship. She sent more pictures of the house and the area and answered our questions. We both figured we had nothing to lose so we signed a one-year lease on the house and agreed to move in a few months. The owner of the house became a great source of information on all things Panama — and our first Panamanian friend who is still our cherished friend.

Remarkably our last few months in the US went smoothly, like it was all meant to be. Our house sold in a few weeks and Toyota bought back both our cars. Despite owing money on both vehicles, after the payout we walked away with just under $10,000. After we packed up our stuff, it was off to a shipping container for a voyage across the sea. We said our goodbyes and left with six suitcases to embark on the adventure of a lifetime.

Clyde suggested that I start writing a blog about our adventures. We thought it would be a great way for our kids and friends to follow along on our journey. Our kids can't be bothered to read it but some of our friends and family do. The most amazing part of the blog has been the hundreds of strangers who found it looking for information on Panama. Some have become friends who now live here, others are still thinking about it and still others are living vicariously through us.

"Moving to a foreign country is not for everyone, but for those willing to embrace the change and take the plunge, the rewards can be life changing. We're thankful every day for our new life, new friends and new experiences living in Panama."

The date was September 3, 2011, which was also Clyde's 57th birthday. Upon arriving in Panama City our plan was to meet our new landlady in one of the huge city malls. We followed her to our rental house, about a 45-minute drive outside of Panama City. As we drove through the gates of the tiny development Clyde nervously said, "Oh dear, what have we gotten ourselves into?" I said, "Well you wanted to live among the locals so here we are."

The house was just as nice as it looked in the photos but since the electric and water were not on yet, we decided to head to Coronado to spend the night at a hotel.

It was late and we were exhausted after a long day of travel, not to mention stressed over moving to another country. Clyde showed his passport at the hotel to the desk clerk as he paid for the room. We carried our luggage to the room then walked to a nearby grocery store for some snacks before retiring to our room for the evening. A while later Clyde panicked that he didn't remember picking up his passport and realized it was gone. We traced our steps back to the hotel lobby where the clerk insisted she did not have his passport. Despite searching the parking lot, in and around the car and the grocery store, it was nowhere to be found.

We had no local cell phones, no Internet, no friends, didn't know the language and now Clyde had no form of identification. It was like we didn't exist or could have fallen off the face of the earth and no one would have known. I felt so utterly alone and afraid. This is not what I signed up for. I was too old to start over again with absolutely nothing, but starting over is what we were doing. It was just the two of us now and we had only each other to rely on for this next chapter of our lives.

The next morning I woke up feeling like a newborn coming into the world for the first time. We knew nothing and no one, and the people around us spoke another language that we didn't fully understand. Where would we go to buy groceries, household items, curtains, utensils, or anything else? How would we get our electric, Internet and water connected or our trash picked up? Yes we were confused, but thankfully my brave husband led the way.

Over the next few days we became acquainted with our new home, our neighborhood and stores. As the weeks turned into months, we became familiar with shopping, eating out and how to get everything hooked up at the house. Eventually our stuff arrived from Texas and our house felt like our home.

About six months later while visiting a friend in Chame, Panama, we noticed a house for sale. Chame sits in the "dry arch" of Panama, an area that gets much less rain than the rest of the country. By this time we had made many friends in the pricey beach community of Coronado but couldn't afford house prices there. Clyde called the number on the for sale sign and eventually we bought the house. A Panamanian style fixer-upper, the house was a weekend home for a prominent local family in Panama City.

The four-bedroom, three-bathroom home is approximately 2,000 square feet and sits on an acre of land. We fell in love with the large outdoor entertaining area, the beautifully landscaped gardens, mature fruit trees and out buildings with full bathroom. After negotiations we paid $90,000 for the house. Clyde later remodeled the kitchen adding 28 feet of granite counter top at a cost of only $350, along with teak cabinets for around $2,000. The house is a labor of love that keeps us busy in our retirement years. Since we choose to have no hired help, I'm the maid, Clyde's the gardener and the work keeps us fit and healthy.

That scary day of moving to Panama is behind us now and we're enjoying life with new adventures every day. Making friends has been easy because no one works so everyone has time. Today we have friends from all over the world we never would have met had we not retired to Panama. There are expats here from Canada, Scotland, Germany, Switzerland, England, Costa Rica and many other places.

Moving abroad is not for everyone but for anyone willing to take the plunge, embrace the changes and accept the differences, it can be wonderful.

Why We Chose Panama

Panama offers foreign retirees a residency visa with a bucket load of discounts. They want people who have made their money elsewhere to move here and spend it in return for discounts. Obtaining pensionado status requires a Panamanian lawyer, proof of having a monthly pension for life, legal fees, and trips to the immigration department. But once established it's good for life and allows us to live here for as long as we want and to enter the country as residents instead of tourists.

Some of the discounts are: 50 percent off hotel stays during the week (30 percent on weekends); 25 percent off airfare; 30 percent off bus, boat and train fares; 50 percent off entertainment (movies, theater, concerts); 25 percent off restaurants (15 percent on fast food); 15 percent off hospital bills (if no insurance); 10 percent off prescriptions; 20 percent off medical consults; and 15 percent off dental and eye exams.

Who We Are

We are Clyde and Terry Coles who moved from Corpus Christi, Texas, to Panama in September 2011. Clyde was a firefighter and paramedic for 30 years. I worked as a customer service representative for a medical equipment company before I checked out of the working world. I'm originally from Jersey City, New Jersey, and Clyde originates from Albuquerque, New Mexico. Since I had lived in many part of the US, I figured, "How hard could it be to live in a different country?" Let's just say it's not necessarily hard, just different. Panamanians do things differently than we do in the States. And we have to realize that just because it's different doesn't mean it's wrong.

As a firefighter, Clyde had good health insurance for which the city paid half while he was working. Once he retired, the cost would have been $1,250 per month for the two of us. Adding to that his ex-wife gets a third of his pension, which left us little to live on. It's because of these things that we left the US to find a more affordable place to live. Here in Panama we own our house and car and live comfortably on about $2,000 per month. We have health insurance here for $200 a month in case something major happens. But we've never had to use it. We can see an English-speaking doctor for $15 and a specialist for around $50. I had a hysterectomy here for $4,500 total fees (hospital, doctor, OR and staff) and received wonderful care.

While maintaining US citizenship, we have obtained permanent residency in Panama. We are free to come and go as we please, each time entering the country through the resident line at the airport.

Our biggest challenge in Panama has been the language barrier. With four years of studying Spanish under our belts, we still take weekly lessons and probably always will. And while learning a new language is more challenging as we age, it's also a good thing to keep our minds active.

For the past three years we've been loving our new laid-back lifestyle in Panama. With such close proximity to the equator, the temperatures are the same year round, making it the land of eternal summer. The local people are patient and slow moving, and very little ruffles their feathers. Panamanians work to live instead of living to work like we used to. They are insanely happy people who enjoy the simple things in life. Spending time with family and friends, a little rum, beer, food and music is all they need to be happy.

Moving to a foreign country is not for everyone, but for those willing to embrace the change and take the plunge, the rewards can be life changing. We're thankful every day for our new life, new friends and new experiences living in Panama.

Terry Coles
Age 55
Texas, US / Chame, Panama

Terry Coles was born with a knack for writing but was never published as a freelance writer until after retiring to Panama. Today she writes about the adventures, joys and challenges of expat living and travelling abroad. Her blog is alongthegringotrail.blogspot.com.

The Thousand-Year Crawl

Taylor Bell

He contemplated taking a shower. That famous post-wake stagnation that leaves him mired every day in his mattress. Five simple minutes of staring at the slanted ceiling, his attic apartment feeling particularly confining today. The skylight swallowing everything equally. It was everyone's afternoon, and he felt the selfish tinge of inaction pull him magnetically out of bed.

The seven-step walk to the bathroom felt like a heart attack. All the way through the kitchen/living room/vestibule into what was the closest thing to a literal water closet he had ever seen. He switched on the faucet with indifference and caught a glimpse of himself in the dirtied mirror above the sink. A strange glance, as if his eyes were overflowing with a particular emptiness.

He ran his hand under the water, waiting for it to heat up. He wondered if his eyes had always been so untrustworthy, or if it was only himself in the afternoons that he didn't trust. Neruda came to mind. The water was not heating up. He remembered that he had fallen asleep before he submitted all his online paperwork for the new job. He remembered that he had an appointment to be fingerprinted, one of a million bruises in the bureaucratic body of living abroad.

He remembered he was supposed to mail the old postcards that he'd found in a shoebox at the back of an antique store. They were beautiful postcards. *What was wrong with the water heater?* Most of them had pictures of old French towns lying in ruin after being bombarded by the German army in World War II. He had woken up too late though. The post office would soon close and besides, he hadn't had enough money to take the metro for days.

His to-do list was growing. The shower sputtered, covering his arm in water, and he drew his hand back from the faucet. His toothbrush lay alone, solitary on the sink, lightly stuck to the ceramic by the film that's left after not washing it well. The bristles were overworn. He considered the whole thing to be a sad metaphor.

He had come to Spain to simplify his life, but even waking up had become complicated. All the appointments, meetings, documents, red tape, loneliness, and the slanted ceiling and the claustrophobic water closet. Everyone he knew was racing. Racing to all of those appointments and open houses, but he almost thought he preferred the thousand-year crawl. The hot water was clearly not functioning today.

He thought about the poem he had started writing three nights ago but hadn't finished. What had he done since then? If it was anything at all, significant or mundane, he couldnt remember. What was the poem even about? He peered out the water closet's door into his room. The notebook lay sedentary at the foot of his bed, open and unmoved for the last three days. He reached to turn the water off and walked silently back into his room. He looked at the notebook and thought again about his toothbrush and crawled back into bed.

"If it is true, however, that you leave a piece of your heart in every place you visit, then he believes he left a large piece of his heart in Galicia. Even if nobody understood it, and maybe he didn't understand it either. The vivid memories are a testament to the sentiment though."

The neighbors are arguing again. The woman's favorite word is *basura*. When it's quiet at night, sometimes vague sounds of a child's cries drift in through the skylight. According to the darkness, it is no longer afternoon. What mysterious life, he wonders, lies behind the skin of a fresh-picked peach? The *fruterias* in Spain, he concedes, are unbeatable. Who knew how much flavor South American bananas lacked, or how sweet a ripe strawberry could be? A muffled call for a mother is now the only sound.

His favorite lunch is a chorizo sausage sandwich with Philadelphia cream cheese. It's not lunchtime anymore, but he gets out of bed and goes to the kitchen/living room/vestibule to make the sandwich. He doesn't bother trying to test the water heater.

The faint cries he hears remind him of all the days in the school last year, and he wonders now what's worse: to work too much and hate it, or to have too much free time and hate it? The kids were forest fires some days. Others, they were poets. Their minds and moods were unpredictable, whether they were like the weather depended on nothing as much as a coin tossed in a fountain. The job itself was a true meditation in patience and understanding, or lack thereof.

It is one thing to live in a place where you do not speak the language, he thinks, but it is another thing entirely to live in a place where you can not speak the language. Galicians were complicated. Madrileños, he thinks, will be much simpler. At least he will be able to understand them. One year now between Madrid, Galicia, and Mexico, and his Spanish, albeit spoken with a horribly mixed accent, rides a tandem bike with hope on the tightrope of fluency.

The sandwich is ready now and eaten in the dark. The child no longer cries. He sits in a chair in the kitchen/living room/vestibule and chews slowly. He holds the plate in his lap and as he takes a drink, concedes that the tap water in Spain is also pretty unbeatable. There is no table because there is nowhere to put a table. When it comes down to it, he thinks, there are basically only three levels of fluency in a language:

• The ability to order and discuss food,
• The ability to recount a story,
• The ability to know when you're being fucked with.

He considers himself now to be somewhere between Level 2 and Level 3. Once the school year begins again, he will have money to take the metro. Walking in Madrid isn't so bad though. He enjoys the pace of life on foot, faces slowly passing by like paper boats set afloat at sunrise. Although sometimes his memories are more like the moon: all but sunken by the afternoon. He forgets nearly all the faces because if he didn't, he would be in love all the time with everyone he passed. Life is sometimes better lived at a crawl. Memories are Darwinian. Only the strong ones survive.

If it is true, however, that you leave a piece of your heart in every place you visit, then he believes he left a large piece of his heart in Galicia. Even if nobody understood it, and maybe he didn't understand it either. The vivid memories are a testament to the sentiment though.

The sandwich is long finished, but he remains in the chair. The darkness doesn't bother him. All the children are asleep, and everyone is a child when they sleep because they rest without the waking reminders of all the responsibilities they have that day.

He wonders if anyone came to fix the water heater while he was asleep. He now raises himself from the chair without a table and leaves the glass of tap water on the floor and the plate in the sink. They say that too many dirty dishes are a classic sign of depression. He disagrees. One day at a time, until one day doesn't feel like enough time.

There is a teachers' orientation tomorrow, but he isn't sure if he will go. There were more forms to download and fill in, which he had forgotten about. He wonders what life was like living in another country before words like Schengen and socio-politics and globalization were part of every conversation. Was it luck or fate that bore him outside these specific lines? Now he walks back into his room and mires himself back into his mattress. The school year is about to begin. The notebook is open on the floor at the foot of the bed. He picks it up and reads the unfinished poem.

Taylor Bell
Age 24
US / Madrid, Spain

Belgian Footprints

Any Brasó

Maybe the fact that I was born in an inflatable boat in the short stretch between two islands has motivated my spirit of travelling, or it could be that my particular hero adventurer has guided my steps. I don't remember the exact moment I decided to leave my conventional life behind, pack my bags for the unknown and exchange the comforts of ordinary life for kilometres of adventure, where every day is a short new life.

When I was a little girl, I traded the blue waters of the Mediterranean Sea surrounding the Balearic Islands archipelago for the scale of greys drawing the skyline of the great city of Madrid. When circumstances led my parents to move to the Spanish capital city, I had to say goodbye to Ibiza, the land where I began my greatest journey.

The remembrance of a Bohemian island where nature was the usual background evolved into a modern and agitated reality, in which an elevator carried me up to the sixth floor of my new home. The castles in the sand of my previous life collapsed and transformed into toys. The evenings I had spent playing with my friends in the forest morphed into afternoons watching television at home or movies at the cinema.

For a lot of time I missed life in Ibiza, but step by step the traces of the past started to clear and I started to accept what the present was offering. Madrid turned into my new hometown — the city where I went to school, the one that witnessed my first true love story and taught me that everything in this life is ephemeral, even the worst of all sorrows.

My years of high school ended at the doors of university where I chose to earn a bachelor's degree in tourism. I suppose my hours of scanning the horizon during the old days trying to guess where ships that cruised the sea were headed, together with all the times I used to raise my head and imagine the routes of the planes in the sky, have had a big influence in my decision to point my life in the direction of travel.

Sometimes I believe the desire to explore new places has always been a part of me, but other times I remember the day I decided to become an expat of the world. I was there, a big smile on my face, posing with my schoolmates for the graduation picture. Gowns and mortarboards flooded the main hall of the Universidad Rey Juan Carlos and while my friends went on about their plans and future jobs in travel agencies, airlines and hotels, I already knew my destiny: I wanted to travel into the wild.

Some time before, I had read *In the Skin of a Lion* by Michael Ondaatje, and that was when I knew the direction my compass would point. During my journey through its pages and along with Patrick, the main character, I discovered Toronto in the early 1900s and all those immigrants who anonymously built the city. An image started taking shape in my mind and I knew that someday I would be part of that landscape. The biggest problem we, the people who dream of travelling, usually face is the lack of money. In my case I had spent all my savings on my studies, so I had no funds left for a plane ticket or to cover my living expenses in another country.

I decided to apply for temporary jobs to avoid getting chained to the obligations of a fixed contract, one of those that whisper in your ear: "Don't ever leave me, think about the future..." So for the following two years I jumped from one company to another, carrying out all types of roles in the most diverse positions. From the comfortable chair of a management position in a multinational company to long hours standing in the street dressed up as something stupid with an advertisement on my head, every job was valid as long as I could make my dream come true.

It was a rainy February morning in 2007 when I received a call from my boss. I was covering a maternity leave in one of the most important banks in Spain, and his offer of a permanent job with superb colleagues and excellent working conditions for one flick of a second made me think twice about staying. But my response was categorical. "I wish I would have been half as brave," he told me. That was the precise moment I knew it was time to leave.

In the heat of an emerging world crisis in which not everyone supported my decision, I packed my bags.

I didn't know where my dream was coming from, but somehow it reflected my most important goals in life. I was lucky enough to count on the unconditional support of my family. They made me feel that happiness is real only when shared and even though they knew my decision could separate our paths forever, they laid a carpet in front of me so I could go after what I really wanted. And I did.

Magic becomes real every time a dream comes true, and one afternoon in May the CN Tower dressed in reds, yellows and greens welcomed me to my new life. After that she turned into a symbol of the achievement of my first chimaera, and every night before going to sleep I glanced out my window and stared at her changing lights as they shone upon the city.

Even though I faced some adversities, and there were some tough moments in which everything seemed to be crumbling, Toronto embraced me and showed me its kindest face. It taught me that you can talk to some random person in the street without being introduced first and that you can trust someone who offers to help you in the subway. And most important of all it revealed to me one of the best kept secrets: everything happens for a reason.

I rented a small room in a charming little house in the outskirts of the city and started taking English lessons. I did research on how to legally get a job and the only option was to apply for a working visa. I was told that the government issued special permits for young Europeans looking for some working experience in Canada, so I applied. A few months later, after filling out a million forms and papers, I started to work in a small bakery in which the owner, a Pakistani immigrant who told marvelous stories about his home-land, showed me the secrets for making the very best *balushahi.*

Time flew by and one arbitrary day almost three years later I decided to end my Canadian adventure. I had managed to answer all the questions I was asking myself, so I simply left, leaving behind the land in which I became my own best friend and learned to enjoy the small things.

I have always believed that the true journey is not the one you live, but the one you remember. That great experience provided me with a new life perspective and memories of an unforgettable place where my footprints will remain.

> *"For the first months after my arrival, I suffered because I wasn't able to communicate well enough. Buying something from the pharmacy, using a pocket dictionary in the grocery store to identify a product, or making a phone call while speaking to a doctor so I could fully understand my diagnosis were daily challenges."*

After leaving Toronto I established my residence in Madrid, where for more than two years I wrote for an important travel magazine. It was a stable, happy time when on top of achieving some professional goals, I had a visit from love.

But when you think you hold the reins on your life, free will comes knocking on your door. For work-related reasons he had to follow the track for Brussels, and I stood in the station wondering if I should take the same train or follow my own path.

After thoroughly meditating about it, some months later I packed my bags again and plunged into the abyss of adventure. I exchanged my long hours on Skype and the comfort of job stability for a blank sheet of paper where I would start writing a new story.

I had visited Belgium some time before and I remember that while waiting for my flight back to Spain, I thought it was one of those countries worth only one visit and I would never come back. And life has those paradoxes, I thought, while standing some years later at the arrival terminal of the same airport waiting for bus number 21, which would take me back to the city where I would make my new home.

In the beginning I compared each step in this land with my experience in Canada. Now I had enough funds to cover my expenses for a while, and my airfare wasn't even in the three digits. No visa required, someone was waiting for me and I had a place to stay. Apparently everything was so easy that I wondered where my adventure movie was now.

But soon I realized that this apparent simplicity was a disguise and difficulties resided in much different topics than in my previous journey. Belgium is a linguistically divided country where French and Flemish, and to a lesser extent German, are official languages. And even though Brussels is in a French-speaking region and English is used frequently, bilingualism and even trilingualism are widely spread.

I decided to study French, taking into account it would be the language that would help me find a job.

I also had some previous knowledge of the language as I had taken some lessons at university. I signed up to the Alliance Française and there I met Wuna, a girl with Chinese origins who turned out to be my first friend in my new home.

Our friendship was nearly impossible; she barely spoke some English and our French was still very basic, but we managed to bond and Wuna helped me appreciate my situation. My country was a mere two-hour flight away and as a European citizen, it was very easy for me to move from one country to another within the Schengen area. She was more than 7,000 kilometers away from her country and had to work wonders to obtain her working visa. This was a vital piece of my adaptation process: "there is always someone who has a harder situation in life than you."

For the first months after my arrival, I suffered because I wasn't able to communicate well enough. Buying something from the pharmacy, using a pocket dictionary in the grocery store to identify a product, or making a phone call while speaking to a doctor so I could fully understand my diagnosis were daily challenges.

The day I got an appointment to register in the Commune as a Belgian citizen I realized how disastrous the bureaucratic issues of the main administrative city of the European Union are and how critical communication is every time there is paperwork involved.

In Brussels everything works under a "rendezvous" or appointment system, without which it is close to impossible to do things like opening a bank account. The problem is that this appointment is scheduled without taking into account your working hours, lessons or convenience. Given the way things work, it is not unusual to take a day off work to solve an important administrative issue or take the car to a mechanic.

I once told Mark, our landlord, that it seemed a bit extreme to fix a rendezvous the day he came to fix the door latch, but he didn't listen. At precisely 3:45 in the afternoon a few days later, demonstrating Belgian punctuality, he showed up fully loaded with the necessary tools to get the job done.

Here, the sun rarely shows its face and rain covers the city with a permanent sense of dampness. Summer is frail and during winter, days are short. Life outdoors is rare, and people take relationships in a different manner than what I'm used to. Sometimes I miss being in a cheerful town like Ibiza, a capital with a high average temperature like Madrid, or a big metropolis like Toronto.

Brussels is a city that makes a slow impression. It took me a while to start falling in love with it but one day while strolling down its charming streets and smelling freshly made waffles, I came to terms with it and we finally made our peace.

I had never been able to comfortably move around by bicycle in any other place, and it is wonderful seeing whole families cycling around town, disregarding the cold and the rain. The *brocomptes*, second-hand markets where people sell their old stuff for a cheap price, are a part of the weekend plans. I have also learned to bake the famous Christmas Speculoos cookies.

Being used to consumerist societies in which leisure spins around shopping centers, here instead I find a city crowded with little shops that close early and where the most important thing is that workers have time to spend with their families. This concept is an important aspect of a society in which family plays a vital role.

The geographical situation of Brussels in the exact center of Europe makes it easy to travel around, with cities such as London (through the Eurotunnel), Paris or Amsterdam just two or three hours away by car. Traveling by plane or train are also affordable options. As home to the main European institutions, the European Commission and the European Parliament, Brussels is a melting pot of nationalities. There are those coming from the countries forming the old continent and a great African community that is the outcome of a rich colonial history. All this makes for an interesting city full of expats who fill the town with multicultural color and sound.

The moment I feel ready to take some interviews in French has arrived and although it hasn't been easy, almost two years after I first set foot here I have managed to find a job and start to make a living. The fact that I don't speak Flemish is a constant limitation, and Belgium still hasn't given me a professional opportunity that completely motivates me. I like to think the day will come when the city forgives our beginnings and offers me a motivation and a second reason for staying.

But as time goes by, it shows me there are moments and experiences that change us forever and inspire who we really are. These adventures do not occur at home. A life that is fully lived implies moving from your comfort zone and pushing the limits, exploring new places. A book took me to the place where

I fulfilled my greatest dream, and love has brought me to a city that has opened my eyes. My footprints form a path throughout the world, and my backpack is filling up with little pieces of places that make me the person I am.

I do not know whether Brussels will be a full stop in my story or whether I will start writing a new chapter in another place. Life has always put me in the correct place so far, and I will let it do the same in the coming years. But distance has made me appreciate the place I come from and has created bonds I never thought could exist. It makes me deeply miss the town that saw me grow up, the place where my dreams started to take shape and to where, no matter where I live, how much I travel or how much time I spend abroad, I will always return.

Any Brasó
Ibiza, Spain / Brussels, Belgium

A tireless adventurer, Any travels the whole world bringing unique stories to her radio show "Viaja con Nosotros" and to her travel blog the bohemiantraveller.com. *Currently she combines her position as Sales Manager in a multinational Belgian company with the edition of a travel book for kids.*

An Expat Woman in Greece

Rebecca Hall

What is an expat? I know the dictionary definition: "To withdraw oneself from residence in
one's native country." Okay, so far so good. I had
withdrawn myself from my native country of the UK
and was temporarily settled in Greece. But the term
"expat" conjured up all sorts of other images for me:
being invited to ambassadors' balls with Ferrero Roche
served on gold platters, groups of expats gathered
together, making snide remarks about "the locals."
Was this really me? I was dreading the cliché, and
yet I'd chosen to go abroad and work. Would this be
something I'd have to endure — the downside of trad-
ing in my nine-to-five lifestyle in my country of birth?

The Village

I arrived in Greece one warm September evening in
2008. As soon as I stepped foot outside the Arrivals

Hall and witnessed the chaos surrounding me — the laughter, squabbles and all-round expressiveness of the Greeks, I knew I wanted to be a part of their life, not mix with an exclusively expat crowd. After all, getting under the skin of a culture had always been my motivation for travelling.

This wasn't hard to do in my first year in Greece. I lived and taught English in a small inland town where I was the only foreigner, so no opportunity for those Ferrero Roche balls but more opportunities to meet the locals. Like the old man who owned the heating oil shop two doors away from my flat: he used to make me endless cups of tea. We couldn't understand each other, but we were quite content to just sit in silence, smiling occasionally and nodding whilst slurping the drink proffered. The students I taught were attentive, interested in British culture and hard-working. But life wasn't all rosy.

What started out as a novelty — living and teaching in a small Greek town — soon became my nemesis. I started to feel isolated and lonely. I couldn't continually rely on the old oil shop man for friendship, and whilst the teachers at my school were courteous, they were very family driven and stuck to their own. As a woman, I felt this underlying societal expectation and curiosity; why wasn't I settled down with kids? This couldn't be further from my personality type, but small towns in Greece have many women who've settled down and done just that.

Yet I still loved Greece and wanted to stay. She'd woven a magic spell over me: the coffee lifestyle, not the "drink to get drunk" one like back in the UK. The beauty of the country and forthrightness of the people and their ability to not follow rules in general ironically suited me. And so the following year I secured a job in Athens at a bigger school.

Athens

I met a mixture of people who socialised more, who were similar to me in outlook and who hadn't settled down like "good girls": Greek, British and American. I was now becoming a part of an expat scene, something I had (rather snobbishly) fought so hard against. Yet these British and Americans also had Greek links: husband and family, so I didn't feel as if I were totally immersed in an expat crowd. And even though I lived in the capital city, still no Ferrero Roche balls and more importantly no groups of expats gathering to moan about their adopted country, at least not in my circle. Hmm, things were looking up.

As a single woman living in a capital city, did and do I feel unsafe? Honestly, no. I never did nor still do anything that I wouldn't do in my home country: walk down a dark alley or hang around notorious areas on my own at night (or day). And I often find when travelling on public transport late, locals will strike up conversations. If I feel at all lost, I just ask someone. People are more than happy to offer assistance, particularly the elderly when they see a young(ish) woman on her own. And the younger people like to practice their English.

As for socialising, there is not this cliquey segregation that I often find in the UK: here old and young congregate in the same bars and coffee shops — often together. It's this behaviour that helped me seek out Greek company, or the company of other expats who also appreciate this character trait of my adopted country.

Practicalities

Being from the UK, it was relatively easy to come to Greece, given that we have limited restrictions on movement within EU countries. Yes, there was — and is — a lot of red tape in Greece, but again being from an EU country helps. The currency didn't take too much getting used to and actually, as the UK Pound is an incredibly strong currency, it was beneficial for me changing pounds into euros. I received more for my money.

Public transport in Athens is incredibly cheap (by UK standards). A ticket for a 70-minute journey costs 1 euro 20 cents. Or you can buy a monthly travel pass covering all transport within Athens (except to the airport, and even that's only an 8-euro metro ride or 5-euro bus ride) for 30 euros. And clean! I have been so impressed with the cleanliness of the metro, the blue and red lines (the newest) especially. They have piped music and TV screens in the stations showing the five-day weather report; and the Acropolis metro even has an Elgin Marbles frieze.

Language

This is something that will take me longer to come to grips with. I am a writer and English as a Foreign Language teacher; my primary language on a daily basis is English. Greek is a hard language to learn and I haven't been for lessons. I actually like not understanding fully the chatter that goes on around me. It puts a spring in my step and makes me feel I am truly living my life in a foreign culture. I detest during visits to the UK hearing people on their mobile phones and being able to understand every word! But if I am honest, this is an excuse for my laziness.

Don't get me wrong, I can speak and understand a little Greek, but I'm not as fluent as someone who's been living in the country for as long as I have should be. I get by using my hands a lot and smiling. So far, it seems to work, especially with my elderly neighbours who keep giving me gifts of food and plants for my back garden (they worry I don't eat enough — you know, that poor English girl all alone. They're probably right, my cooking isn't up to scratch either; hence why I love Greek food).

I've lived in Greece for seven years now and divide my time between here and my home country of the UK and yes, whilst I may be considered an expat, I prefer to call myself an Honorary Greek.

Rebecca Hall
Age: early 40s
UK / Greece

You can follow Rebecca on her website: lifebeyondbordersblog.com, *Facebook:* facebook.com/ LifeBeyondBordersBlog, *and Twitter:* twitter.com/BeyondBex. *She is the author of debut novel,* Girl Gone Greek, *available on Amazon.*

"What makes expat life so addictive is that every boring or mundane activity you experience at home is, when you move to a foreign country, suddenly transformed into an exciting adventure. When abroad, boredom, routine and 'normal' cease to exist. And all that's left is the thrill and challenge of uncertainty."
— Reannon Muth

At the Heart of It

Kaleena Stroud

I don't know how I ended up in Buenos Aires, Argentina, but I can tell you the steps that led me here. I can't tell you if this is the place I will spend the rest of my life, but anywhere I have lived and scattered memories under the streetlights and in the clouds overhead will be home. Nobody can say where their final destination will be but sometimes how life turns out is simply unexpected and amazing.

Let me start by saying that I am only in my mid-20s and I haven't been an expatriate for very long. I don't have decades of wisdom from my life abroad to pass along, I haven't encountered all the hardships that I know I will someday, and I have yet to internalize how my decisions will have resurfaced in another, later time. But as I sit here in my apartment in a quiet suburb of an otherwise bustling city, drinking mate with the buzz of a Spanish-dubbed Hollywood film in the background, I feel that I have lived more life than a "normal" counterpart my age — more life than I had planned for myself. I had imagined being in a foreign country many times but I never expected it to happen so soon in life. The difference is that I had little time to mentally prepare for such a big change. I didn't come with years of savings in my bank account, the local language, friends or even any plans. I came for love.

I had freshly graduated college from a four-year university and gone straight into a full-time job as a technical writer for a Fortune 500 company. I was extremely lucky to be in such a position in the troubled economy of California. While grateful and hopeful about my future, I was tired and dreaming of travel. So with graduation gifts and saved money, I booked a two-week trip to Costa Rica, complete with a week stay in a yoga retreat near the Caribbean Sea and some free time in a popular town a few hours away called La Fortuna. I also dreamed up a trip across Western and Northern Europe for that summer.

Traveling or adventuring alone is not as easy or even as exciting as it sounds. What I've learned from talking about my travel plans for so long is that many people are interested and excited by the idea of traveling but not many people will follow through. When I asked friends if they'd join me, they partook in my plans enthusiastically but I knew they were not serious. The common excuses bled out: I can't take time off work, I don't have the money, I don't know where to start, who is going to take care of so-and-so. My mother, who had traveled plenty at a young age, gave me the best advice, which I will now pass along: Plan the trip and the right people will follow or they will already be there. So I did. I began my adventures alone and went to Costa Rica, ready to search inward and look for myself. I ended up finding the love of my life — an Argentinean with whom I've begun my new life in his hometown of Buenos Aires.

How it happened? On my last night in La Fortuna before heading home to California, I met Eduardo. Being a solo traveler forced me to talk to people because I didn't have anyone by my side, and it forced me to be spontaneous because I didn't have a reason to make plans. And in that sweet and frightening place outside my comfort zone, I met the person who changed my life forever. He asked me to go dancing with a group of travelers in the same hotel and I agreed. We truly had a movie-esque night and kept in touch through email. Then he visited California and in one short week we fell in love and made our long-distance relationship work until I could visit his country.

The summer arrived shortly after this and I was ready for Europe. I by no means had a lot of money. I worked full time, saving every penny I could. I held onto my 1996 Ford Mustang which broke down many times throughout the years and I lived in an apartment with three other people to keep rent low. As a new graduate, I could have and really wanted to buy a new, reliable car or get a place of my own. But I saved it all to travel. More specifically, I also saved points on my credit card to use toward travel, rented out my room via Craigslist while I was away, budgeted my trip, and lived on only the essentials. And along the way, my newly graduated friend and roommate decided to come with me. My mother's advice had worked.

But how do these trips compare to actually moving to a different country? I said that I would tell you what led me to where I am today. Little by little, I learned to break free and embrace a different way of life. My point is that it doesn't have to be a huge leap all at once. I spent six weeks backpacking through Europe — Belgium, Holland, Germany, England, Ireland and France — but soon my heart weighed heavily and I quickly decided I had to go to Argentina to see my long distance love. Visiting Argentina was the simplest trip to plan because I had most everything taken care of by Eduardo. But soon we found ourselves faced with the inevitable question of "here or there?" Due to the logistics of culture, money, and visas, along with many personal reasons from both of us, I moved from California to Argentina.

It's been a good choice because the US dollar goes a long way here and obtaining a visa is quite simple with just a background check and some cash. On top of that, I don't feel separated from any type of culture in California. I do not have a home base there so the things I miss are intangible, like friends and family. But being an expat these days is quite cozy! I have Skype, email and social media to keep connected and everyone has been very supportive. Argentina is full of culture and it's been fun to adapt to new traditions and customs like drinking mate instead of coffee, greeting with a kiss on the cheek, expressing emotions with hand gestures, an insane passion for futbol and a dear love for family. Some things were difficult to adjust to like the chaotic streets, using common insults as jests toward friends, and the crazy drivers that put New York City to shame. But overall, the tranquil lifestyle is delightfully contagious.

One of the hardest things when I began to travel and then start an expatriate life was giving up my career — or at least putting it on hold. I was the first in my family to graduate college as I held part-time jobs and unpaid internships to help with expenses and gain field experience. Years of studying with an end-goal catered to a career-oriented economy and the pressure of a status-obsessed society, I felt the next step was to get a full-time job and support myself. When everybody around me was climbing the corporate ladder, I wanted to climb too. But somehow, somewhere in my heart I never felt that was the ultimate direction for me. The following poem struck a chord with me when I was struggling to believe in myself to travel because of the constant fight between wanderlust and the need for stability:

My heart wants roots
My mind wants wings.
I cannot bear
Their bickerings.
— E.Y. Harburg

What my expatriate life has shown me is that as soon as I began to focus on something more than materialism and career, I quickly became rich in friendship and lucky in love. Here in Argentina, I have been free to focus on whatever I am passionate about, not just what I happen to be good at — and the right opportunities have spilled before me. The anxiety was strong in the beginning but I trusted in the adventure.

When you stop using excuses to hold you back from going, the momentum is unstoppable. I am living life in a different culture and speaking a language other than my native tongue every day. When you're an expat, every day is a choice to be different, to learn and to follow a passion. And every day I choose love over comfort. I haven't let anyone tell me what an expat should be like in age, in wealth, or in confidence. An expat who might be hopeful, desperate for change or scared can also be an inspiration in the eyes of a local who could only ever dream of doing what an expat has done. I believe taking this leap has put my heart and mind in a peaceful compromise — now I have been given roots and wings.

Kaleena Stroud
Age 25
California, US / Buenos Aires

Kaleena is a graduate of California State University, Long Beach, cultivating her skills as a freelance writer in Buenos Aires and discovering the heart of a life abroad. You can find her at: www.nomadscratchpad.com and follow her on Instagram @nomadscratchpad.

A Second Life:
Full Circle – Hungary
to Indonesia and Back

Tamás Inczédy

I was 79, lying on a bed surrounded by my huge family. All my children and grandchildren were standing around, every face as long as a fiddle. Obviously I was going to die at any moment.

To be frank I cared neither about the pain displayed on my relatives' faces nor the fact that my life was coming to its end. Instead I was really upset at the sum of my life. In that bed I had to admit that during my entire life I had never done the things I really wanted to. I felt I would not let myself down like that again if I could somehow have another chance.

I was swimming in sweat and my heart was racing when I woke up. At 26 years of age I had a nightmare that saved my life. My decision was made right away, and it was my best one ever — a journey to explore the world.

I was ready to burn bridges and leave everything behind but preparations took time. For I was out of money and needed tropical vaccines and information. Willing to face these technical issues, I did my best to get through them and first started researching and applying for scholarships. This was the point when mediocracy attacked me in a most sneaky way. As weeks passed while preparing for the journey, my life somehow became wonderful. Indeed I started to enjoy it. I did not change my mind about the journey itself but was about to push the date of departure. After a while the whole travel plan seemed blurry and childish.

I guess there were two things responsible for my feelings: 1) some negative circumstances were almost at an end and literally everything in my surroundings, even the tiniest details, became precious, and 2) the last shot effect. How shall I explain this? Look at it this way: Trees blossom in the most amusing and intense way during their last spring. They feel it is their last shot before death.

At the end of the day you can blame circumstances but that won't make your life any better. If it is about your life, you are the one who must act to change your circumstances, no one else. I had to force myself to remember that nightmare in order to carry on. Finally I quit my white-collar job and gave up my hobby of being a small-town rock star.

However, there still remained a step I never took — something I totally messed up and still feel sorry about. The most difficult thing was a personal issue in which I regret to say, I failed. What happened? Well, I left behind my girlfriend without letting her know I was going to leave with another. Yes, I know, I was an ass. I am sorry about it 1,000 times and paid big time for it as well. I do not mean to complain; that is what I deserved, and life I believe is somehow fair in the long term.

All in all I almost turned back, but I finally left my homeland, Hungary, to explore the real world.

I ended up in Jawa, Indonesia, one of the most beautiful places on Earth.

I imagine the following things happen to most expats. In the first three months I was feeling like a tourist. I mostly enjoyed my days, appreciated new things and had some kind of cultural shock as most of us do when diving into the unknown. After that I started to have a daily routine, and the country's weird things were neither that awkward nor that awesome anymore.

A half year changed me a lot and as I got deeper and deeper into the foreign and strange culture and language, I somehow did not want to move or travel farther even though my original plan was to get to those beautiful islands of New Zealand.

In a couple of years as much as it is possible for a Western person, I became one of the locals. I loved that life — the simplicity, the way of thinking and mostly everything.

Then came those days of the volcano eruptions. The evacuation line was next to my house and those nights I slept with my motorbike helmet on.

I decided to mess up life once again and go to Australia, from which I left during the Brisbane flood.

Back to Indonesia with a plan this time. I proposed and got engaged to my Indonesian girlfriend and headed back to Hungary to visit and introduce her to my family. Then we stayed. We have been married for three years now and have a beautiful little princess, our daughter.

The funny thing is that before, the devil wanted to keep me back while the angels whispered the magic word 'go'. Now I am a family man, a father. The devil says ignore your responsibilities and go, and the angels want me to stay. I guess all I can do is listen to both of them and be myself.

Tamás Inczédy
Age 33
Hungary /Indonesia / Budapest

Tamás grew up in a forester's lodge and graduated in economics. He is author of three novels, Cyclopedia of Nonexisting Words, Mansoup, *and* The Juggler, *and several shorts. He also writes tales not only for kids. 'Second life' is his first work available in English.*

The Journey Here

Ed O'Connor

In retrospect the journey Here began in 2010 when
Bill, our friend from church, mentioned he was
thinking about traveling to another country and possibly buying a home. We were disenchanted with the
United States and the oppressive government, which
we saw as only getting worse. In fact my wife Olga,
who was born in Siberia and raised in the former
Soviet Union, said she felt she had more freedom in
the Soviet Union than in the US.

Bill went to Panama and indeed purchased a beautiful property in a most exclusive area. He and his
wife invited us to visit, and in March 2011 we winged
our way to Panama City, Panama. After a 90-minute
commute, we arrived at Bill's new home — a large,
beautiful complex complete with pool and swim-up
bar in a gated community in Coronado Beach.

We spent 10 days in Panama and after returning to
the US really had something to think about. We knew
we could not afford anything near that lifestyle, plus the

weather was hotter than the hinges of hell there, so we searched online for an alternative location in Panama and found Boquete. It was in the mountains so the climate was bearable and it was much more affordable. We bought books about Panama and retiring abroad and studied what we could find on the Internet. We both had jobs so there was no real urgency to do anything or make plans, but it was fun to dream. Then came April Fool's Day.

On April 1, 2011, my supervisor at work told me the company no longer required my services. I thought it was an April Fool's joke. It definitely was not. At age 64 I was unemployed. To put the proverbial icing on the cake, the Tuesday after Labor Day, September 6, 2011, five months after losing my job, we lost our home and possessions in the flood waters of Tropical Storm Lee.

After applying for 101 jobs and having but one interview, I figured there had to be something better somewhere. So back to the books and the Internet. We noticed that the cost of living was rising in Panama and since we would have only one income, my social security, Panama was no longer an option. Now what? After months of more research we decided on Here.

We departed from Harrisburg International Airport on December 11, 2012, with nothing but faith and nine pieces of luggage. Nearly 3,000 miles later we were Here. Ironically we arrived on 12/12/12 at 12 noon. So where in the world is Here ?

Here is Cuenca, Ecuador, South America. Cuenca has been consistently named as one of the top locations in the world in which to retire and after living here for almost two years, I must wholeheartedly agree.

We made a move that many people said was foolish, insane and other adjectives I cannot use. Probably the biggest response and question is, "Why would you leave the No. 1 country in the world and move to a third-world country?" I have been asked that by friends, relatives, tourists, and print and video journalists. What an easy question to answer! After working for nearly 50 years including four years in the military, I was totally disillusioned with the US at every level.

Is the US No. 1? You bet it is — No. 1 in the world in at least 20 aspects, some of which include: the largest prison population on the planet; the highest percentage of obesity; the highest divorce rate; more police officers; more money spent on health care as a percentage of gross domestic product; more people on pharmaceutical drugs; the highest trade deficit; more military bases; and the largest debt of any country.

This city, Cuenca, is an interesting and beautiful place. It was founded in 1557. Four rivers traverse the city, and many small neighborhood parks and well-manicured linear parks with bicycle/walking paths border the rivers. The parks also have the outdoor version of indoor exercise equipment. You can bike/walk from one side of the city to the other on the river paths. Cuenca lies one degree from the equator, hence you would assume it would be very hot. Not so. The city is 8,300 feet above sea level so the weather is wonderful. I equate the climate to late summer or early fall in Pennsylvania. Keep in mind that in the southern hemisphere the seasons are reversed. Summer temperatures (Fahrenheit) are in the 70s during the day and 60s at night. In winter the temps run about 10 degrees less. We have no heating or air-conditioning in our apartment.

Because of the altitude, the air is thinner and has less oxygen, affecting about 25 percent of tourists and new residents. The main symptoms are light-headedness and tiring quickly, but one soon becomes acclimated. I never experienced the problem, but Olga did for about the first 10 days. The altitude's big plus is insects — there are very few. In Pennsylvania we had to bathe in insect repellent when walking by the river unless we wanted to be a black fly and mosquito buffet.

Having grown up in small-town America, I never liked cities and always felt uneasy in them. In fact on a visit to New York City, I experienced my only panic attack and had to go to Central Park so I could breathe. So when deciding to live in a city of 550,000, I had serious trepidation. My fears were vanquished on our first day here. The city has a small-town feel and I feel totally comfortable walking the streets day or night.

Cuenca is the cultural capitol of Ecuador and there is much to do and see. There is a plethora of museums, art galleries and historical sites. The largest museum, a theatre and some Inca ruins are a 10-minute walk from our apartment. There is the Cuenca Symphony Orchestra, the youth symphony orchestra and the youth orchestra whose performances are free.

There are four universities and we volunteer at one, Cuenca University, to aid students in speaking English. There are 52 cathedrals in the city, the oldest one was built in 1567. Most are magnificent architectural masterpieces. A new state-of-the-art planetarium recently opened and was designed to look like the planet Saturn complete with rings. Holidays and parades abound. One of the longest parades in the world is the Christmas Parade (Paseo del Nino Parade) on December 24. Approximately 50,000 people participate and about 200,000 view the parade. The *Cuencanas* are happy, friendly and laid-back. Their attitude seems to be that they work to live, not live to work. The crime rate is very low. Unemployment is low. Thousands of Ecuadorians who left Ecuador to work in the United States are returning after years — mainly to Cuenca.

There is much construction and renovation throughout the city. A new $230-million light rail system is being built to be completed this year. A $700-million, 50-kilometer (30-mile), six-lane highway with 11 bridges around Cuenca is being planned. Two of the bridges will be the longest in South America.

Our new city of residence is not perfect. Yes, we have encountered problems and there are things we find challenging or do not like. The biggest difficulty is the language, whigh is Spanish. Period. Olga and I have been studying it and Spanish will be Olga's fifth language! Learning Spanish is not easy but we are guests here. When we arrived, I knew two Spanish words: *cerveza* and *baño* — "beer" and "bathroom." Fortunately my vocabulary has expanded since then.

Getting our permanent visas was a difficult process. It took six months. The immigration office kept changing the rules and requirements. What was correct yesterday was not correct today. It was an extremely frustrating experience that required much patience. Apparently bureaucrats are the same everywhere. I understand the visa process is easier now.

No city is without annoyances and in Cuenca, cars create some of them. Car alarms are the bane of tranquility. Most cars have them and they all sound the same, from a 2015 Ferrari to a 1985 Yugo. And car horns. When the traffic light turns green, drivers lay on their horns, even drivers 10 cars back. Car turn signals are another story — they are rarely used. Too bad the horns don't activate the turn signals.

Traffic lights and stop signs seem to be suggestions — pedestrians beware! There are many street dogs so you must be alert when walking. Graffiti can be another irritation, but despite these annoyances I would still rather live here than in the US.

How many times have I heard, "But, Ed, aren't living conditions primitive?" Well, not exactly. We live in a new 1,616-square-foot apartment that has three bedrooms, two bathrooms, dining room, living room, kitchen and laundry. There are ceramic tiled floors throughout, except for the bedrooms which have hardwood floors. The kitchen has a breakfast bar that seats six, and all the kitchen countertops are marble. The apartment is big enough and has more storage space than we will ever fill. We have two skylights and a modern security system. And the monthly rent — $350.

"But, Ed, is the water safe to drink?" Studies show that the water in Cuenca has been rated the best water in South America. We drink the water straight from the tap.

What a joy it is not to own a vehicle! No payments, no gasoline, oil, tires, maintenance and no insurance. Since I am over 65 I can take a bus any place in the city for 12 cents. For those under 65 the cost is 25 cents. Taxi fares run between $2 and $3. If one owns a car here, gasoline is $1.48 per gallon and diesel fuel is $1.03 per gallon.

A lunch at one of the local restaurants consisting of a bowl of soup, large platter, juice and dessert costs $2. I walk across the street for a haircut/beard trim: $2. The only tax I pay is 12 percent on purchases but since I am over 65, I get all the tax I have paid back by submitting a form with my receipts. I am living tax free. If one uses the credit unions, (cooptivas), the rate of interest on a certificate of deposit is between 8 and 10 percent.

Since we have to pinch every penny until Lincoln's eyes water, I keep careful track of our expenses. Yes, the dollar is the currency so there is no worrying about exchange rates. Here is what my monthly expenses have averaged the past 28 months:

- Electricity (includes trash pickup three times weekly): $12.70
- Water: $6.61
- Propane (for hot water, clothes dryer and stove/oven): $4.64
- Internet/Phone: $30.11
- Transportation: $17.40

Two categories of items considerably more expensive here are automobiles, which are roughly 30 percent more, and electronics, which can be as much as double the price in the states. To help remedy the high price of electronics, a new television manufacturing facility is being built and a new cell phone factory has just opened. A new smart phone will be $85.

"But, Ed, I suppose when you are sick you go to a medicine man?" No, I go to the medical clinic that also has a dentist and massage therapist. A visit there is $15. Medical and dental tourism is flourishing in Cuenca and one can certainly see why. Price and service. For example, people can come here for dental implants and pay 75 percent less than in the US. Most doctors and dentists here are trained in the US or Europe.

Since I have been in Cuenca, I have lost 30 pounds and three inches from my waist. My blood pressure and blood sugar are the best they have ever been. I attribute those better numbers to a healthier lifestyle and the fact that the fruits and vegetables are seldom exposed to pesticides and there are no genetically modified foods, (GMOs). The animals are free range, there is no animal "warehousing" and they are not shot full of growth hormones, steroids and antibiotics.

There is government health insurance but it is not mandatory. One can purchase government insurance, private insurance or no insurance. My government insurance premium is $73.73 monthly and for an added dependent, the additional cost is $10.12. Government insurance covers medical, dental, prescription and hospitalization with no deductibles or copays.

That's my story and I'm stickin' to it. Now you know where Here is, how we got Here and why Here is where we intend to stay.

Ed O'Connor
Age 68
Pennsylvania, US / Cuenca, Ecuador

Abroad in Argentina

Stephen Seifert

The subtle laughter of children playing at a distant
school is interrupted by obscene whistles of an
old windowless train as it arrives slowly to one of its
many stops. Car horns resonate from all corners of
my neighborhood, remarks of anxious drivers stuck
in traffic. Cheap yet reliable motorcycles and mopeds
with unsettling powerfully loud mufflers whip by as
people tango in and out of each other in passing on
busy street corners.

I am sitting patiently, feeling the warm spring sun
on my face as I watch a one-legged pigeon hop from
table to table harassing tea sippers and coffee enthusi-
asts as they gossip about the day's events and national
politics. I watch the pigeon, the pigeon examines the
people and we all mutually experience it all. This is
their home, a wondrous utopia of enriched cultures
that is Argentina. A proud country beset in South
America that is now my home, and each morning I
ponder how I ended up here in the first place.

I would like to say that it was an easy transition, a short journey that has led me to a home I share with my wife among the many towering apartment buildings within Capital Federal, Buenos Aires. I traded happy hour in the comfort of my small mountain town in Oregon for 6 p.m. tea time in a bustling city with people from all over the world and all walks of life. The journey that has led me to Buenos Aires and my beautiful Argentinian partner began one summer off from college while on a short break in Riviera Maya, Mexico.

Once a world traveler always a world traveler some would say, and I would graciously agree. I spent the summer soaking up the sun on the beaches of Isla Mujeres and tramping around the many majestic and ancient Mayan ruins that protrude from the jungle canopies of the Yucatan. It was a pilgrimage that led me back to Oregon where I finished my studies, packed my bags and was off to make a new life in Mexico, a truly awe-inspiring country. In retrospect it wasn't far from the United States, a landing pad I could escape from if things didn't go the way I intended.

When I had enrolled for my first classes at Southern Oregon University, I wasn't what you would call a traditional student. I began my formal education after spending the majority of my 20s in the US Army where I would find myself far from home and navigating through life in warm sandy places like Iraq and Afghanistan. I had always liked the sandy beaches and though the Euphrates had its own assortment of riverside beaches, I preferred something a little more tropical. The Caribbean was ideal and as a budding anthropologist, I felt drawn to the traditional culture and life ways that still appeared intact among the Mayan people.

After my maiden voyage to Mexico and finishing my degree, I forwent the audaciously boring commencement that was set for the summer to come. I left on Superbowl Sunday and arrived at Isla Mujeres just in time to watch the second half of the game with a group of unquestionably intoxicated expats and tourists waving hands about, boldly sporting Mexican style ponchos embedded with their favorite team's logo.

When you decide to live in another country, you always miss home in certain ways and I have often found myself reverting to sports and food to comfort my wandering soul. It's definitely not always easy, but nothing really is and living as an expat becomes an ever-changing educational experience with little to no learning curve. I have found myself just winging it on more than one occasion in Mexico and most definitely in Argentina.

When living abroad it's important to stay busy. Working odd jobs or participating in something you might be good at helps you meet locals and other expats. It can often provide an overall fun experience with people you might later build a relationship with. At the least you will develop a small network of expats and locals who share common interests. I have had several jobs since moving to other countries, and they have all proven to be exciting experiences and exceptional networking opportunities. Though I consider myself semi-retired, I have found solace in the various part-time jobs I have undertaken.

Reading books on the beach and going for walks around the local neighborhood do get boring after a while, and I always enjoy new and exciting journeys of freelance or part-time gigs. Having a savings is always a good idea when moving to another country. However, working is beneficial to your mental and physical health as well as your bank account depending on your lifestyle. I have always lived meagerly and my part-time gigs have included English teacher, physical trainer, marketing director, paddle board instructor, tour guide, property salesman, freelance writer, and consultant; all of which have kept my lifestyle afloat.

I met Ceci in Playa del Carmen, Mexico, while staying in a hostel after moving out of my apartment in Tulum. The reason I moved is a valuable lesson in expat living; I failed to do my research and was paying rent on a studio apartment with few amenities when for the same price I could have had a two-bedroom apartment on the beach next to a golf course. Research is the key to living as an expat in any country. Always keeping your ear to the ground and getting in with locals can save you time and money. I was foolish but learned from my mistakes and destiny pointed me in the direction of love.

Ceci was from Argentina and worked at the hostel full time after spending the winter season in Lake Tahoe. She was an expat in her own right, and we shared several weeks of limited communication since my Spanish was at a beginner level and her English the same. With use of hand signals and smiles from across the desk where she attended to the hostel's guests, we were able to build a relationship. I would bring her peanut M&Ms and Coca Cola daily as little offerings of my affection. Knowing the language before you go or learning quickly is extremely important to navigating a country in which you wish to live. I am still learning the Spanish spoken in Argentina, a fast rambling of unfamiliar words that were not in my high school Spanish class.

We fell in love despite our communication barriers at the start and decided that we would spend as much time together in our lives as we could. Moving to Argentina was not easy for me. Dinner is late and if you are hungry before 8 p.m., good luck finding a place that serves a hardy meal at what would be my normal feeding time. The difference in culture is often vast, and the loud morning honking from anxious drivers waking up every dog in the barrio is something I am still coping with.

We have been living in Buenos Aires for over two years now and I'm finally settling into my writing career and the city, which so boldly never sleeps. Ceci and I, once a family of two, are now three, with the arrival of our son Viggo. The simple act of choosing a child's name when living abroad is a definite indicator to your expat life. Ceci is Argentinian and I an American, thus the woes of finding the perfect name that represent both cultures became a daily topic. We adapted, just as all expats must adapt while assimilating into a new dynamic culture.

I have learned how to do many things that I had once had the comfort of paying for, and patience has become a virtue in more ways than I can count. Certain sauces and foods I had enjoyed at home are not available to me here and as an expat it's something one must learn to deal with. I have become more vibrant in the kitchen, creating dishes and sauces that were dear to my heart in the US and it has helped me realize the importance of a simpler, more traditional lifestyle. Saturdays or Sundays are for family, and my fiancée's family often gathers in the home of her grandmother where they break bread together almost every weekend.

The key virtue to have as an expat living abroad, far from home and comforts, is patience. Being patient as an expat will ease your transition and help you see your new home and culture objectively. Breathe it all in and enjoy a simpler and maybe slower lifestyle than you are accustomed to. I went from a small Oregon town with neighbors a mile down the road to the bustling streets of Buenos Aires, but life is oddly simpler than before.

The experience of living in Argentina has not always been ideal, but the experience of living abroad is a beautiful and wondrous journey that has made me a more kind and patient man. My objective approach and openness has led me to see the beauty in a one-legged pigeon hopping from table to table under the warm Argentinian sun.

Stephen Seifert
Age 35
Oregon, US / Buenos Aires, Argentina

Stephen Seifert is a professional writer of fiction and nonfiction. Stephen's passion for travel and culture fuels his worldly adventures and experiences. He is currently located in Argentina, spending his days with his wife Ceci and son Viggo.

This Old World
Is a New World

Michael Sinding

We moved from Canada to Europe in late 2006. We've lived in Ireland, Germany, Austria and The Netherlands (multiple cities in some countries) and held around a dozen different jobs between us. Another move may be around the corner.

Why one does anything, especially something big, is always a complicated question because causes are complicated. Even when you know the reasons, they are often of various sizes, moving at various speeds along intricately tangled channels like some machine designed by Dr. Seuss and operated by a team of long-necked birds and colourful cats.

So We Went because of some conjunction of direct causes and enabling conditions. Three key things: One, jobs. Prospects in multiple countries encouraged us to take the leap. Two, we weren't deeply tied to where wc were. Three, the prospect of adventure was irresistible. Then, as they say, way leads on to way.

The tipping point was when we both got European job offers at around the same time. Melissa was head-hunted by a big tech company in Dublin; I was awarded a postdoctoral fellowship by a German research foundation. Granted, these positions were in different countries, and we didn't know how we would get them to mesh (Weekends here and weekends there? Live in France and commute in both directions?). But they were much closer to each other than either was to Canada. A door opened and we realized we could step through. The Old World would be our New World. We figured we could always come back if it didn't work out. But it was then or never.

How did things come to that? By 2005 we were getting settled into careers and homes in southern Ontario but we weren't *quite* settled. Both 2002 and 2003 had been big years. We'd bought our first house, gotten married and I'd finished my PhD. We were close to family and friends, had our routines and attachments and enthusiasms, and expected things would continue in roughly predictable directions within a reasonable geographic compass.

In 2003 I'd been granted a Canadian federal postdoc fellowship, so I worked on a research project while also learning the ropes as an itinerant English literature teacher, aiming at the tenure track. Melissa was an IT manager, clambering the corporate ladder. One of us always had a good position and sometimes we both did.

By 2005 a big change pushed our roots deeper, and another quite pulled them up. One was our own stately pile into which we threw money, time and effort: a rambling century home (presumably haunted) with triple-red-brick walls, hardwood floors, probably 15 rooms, three fireplaces, speaking tubes, gigantic beech trees and sprawling lawns. We discovered it in Tillsonburg, a little tobacco town, made an offer and were amazed it was accepted.

If we'd had kids then, that may well have planted us there. But we didn't feel done yet. And the job situation remained fluid. My postdoc ran out and I was still at the application game. The humanities had their crises (funding cuts) and the tech companies had theirs (booming chaotically). For us too much flux, not enough bucks. We considered options. One came through: Melissa was offered a job in Boston. Lucky us: I was soon offered a starting job at Boston University.

But just as we were getting settled there, the Old World called. Germany held out a postdoc to me; Ireland reached back to Boston and headhunted Melissa. We're your new world, they said.

What else helped? Globalization, integrating nations by opening borders to trade and people. It's probably easier to be an expat now than ever before. We rode that wave. I put it down to information and communications technology. You can effortlessly get much information about any place in the world and communicate with anyone anywhere. You can contact employers and officials anywhere, arrange travel from anywhere, learn any language from anywhere. In many ways, you can work from anywhere. To grasp the shock of the sea-change, compare international communication via expensive and noisy landlines, snail-mail and travel agents.

Our European roots and European Union unification have been decisive. I was able to acquire Irish citizenship and we could live EU-wide.

Our work turned out to be highly mobile. You can research, teach, manage and be artisans anywhere. Professions tied to localities cannot easily work elsewhere (e.g. local laws and regulations).

And I suppose we share a romantic streak. We like adventures. How much could we squeeze out of life?

So the leap followed a happy convergence of sound practical and financial motivations, absence of obstacles, and personality. But we remember best the thrill, the giddy sense that a hole had opened in the universe and we were being invited to step through it. How could we not?

Nuts and bolts

Moving

Radical moves mean giving up all you can stand to give up. This is both horrible and exhilarating.

We've had two kinds of moves: arranged by the employer and arranged by ourselves. Each has pros and cons. Our self-managed moves (to Germany, Austria, The Netherlands) involved much less property, distance and complexity. We went with small movers and small cars, or planes and trains. Again, the Internet makes all of this immeasurably easier: we can search for lodgings (actually see the place and its neighbourhood), sell property, find movers (get quotes and bookings) and communicate with government offices and utilities.

Money

It's expensive to move to new countries and to return back overseas (we visit once or twice per year). It's complex to reorganize legal and political ties. You may need accountants. On the other hand, the cost of living in Europe seems much lower than in Canada. Rents are roughly comparable, but groceries are much more affordable.

Languages

One huge proviso is that you need to know at least one of your new country's languages. In Germany we were a bit traumatized by how lost we were at first, how hard it is to learn the language and how much you need it to do the simplest things. I would estimate it took six months of immersed learning before I could have a basic conversation (and I like languages). Two years is a standard estimate for time to moderate fluency.

What would happen if we had some emergency? I knew that 112 is Germany's 911 but if I had needed to call, I wouldn't have been able to explain a damn thing. Accomplishing anything official (registering residence, renting a flat, getting a car and insurance and repairs, etc.) was tragicomic. We signed many papers without really understanding them. We relied on pictures to interpret our world (e.g. while shopping). You must accept that you will feel stupid for a while. Mark Twain's essay, "The Awful German Language", may help you get through dark times.

But different countries are different. In The Netherlands, almost everyone speaks some English and most speak it very well. This makes it easier to live there but harder to learn Dutch.

How to learn? Take classes if possible. ICT helps here too: find lessons on CD or online and practice by reading news, magazines and books; watching TV and videos; and listening to podcasts. We watched reruns of *The Simpsons* in German ("Ausgezeichnet," says Mr. Burns, pressing his fingertips together). You no longer need to hunt for this stuff in libraries; you open your computer and it's there. But there's no substitute for speaking with native speakers.

I read *Grimms' Fairy Tales*, watched videos from *Der Spiegel* and listened to German and Dutch lessons while jogging. I discovered the dtv bilingual book series with German on one page and English on the facing page, fairy tales, and stories and poems by Poe, Wilde, Shakespeare, etc. (They're intended for Germans so they're German translations of English originals.)

Swings and roundabouts

There has been a steady flow of trials and marvels. At times we've felt we made a gigantic mistake, and in a low-level panic wished we were "back home". This comes from running low on employment and money, but also from social and cultural factors. While most of our employer-hosts have been welcoming, our first ones in both Dublin and Germany neglected us inexcusably. They invited us over, accepted our work and left us to our own devices when we arrived. We were drones, not colleagues. No doubt they were very busy and all; who isn't? They had no concern for us and we felt no loyalty in return. Within a year in Ireland we decided to go to Germany and Melissa decided to become a jeweler. We've never looked back. Her stuff is carried in shops and online, and we often take part in markets (Amsterdam's are superb), which are great places to sample local talent, meet other makers and join new venues. We're gaining circles of colleagues and customers. I've had better results in European than North American academia. (I'm like David Hasselhoff; they love me more in Germany than in America.)

A few short episodes from our new homelands flesh out this balance of ups and downs.

Ireland

The flats and furnishings in Ireland are for wee people: tiny stairways, tiny yard, tiny fridge, tiny oven, tiny shower and sink. I'd crack my elbows every time I showered and leave a puddle every time I washed over the sink. We longed for Canadian vastnesses.

The pubs. Some are works of art and real public houses where families gather with kids and all at certain times. Our local in Bray had a children's section with a toy box.

Germany

Our first experience of Germany threw us into some of the best of what the country offers. Marburg is a stupendously well-preserved medieval town in a pine valley (the rumour is that exactly one bomb fell on it in WWII). It cannot have looked much different during the Reformation. Cobblestone streets lined with half-timbered houses wind around the steep central hill, which is topped by a fortress-castle with grounds and gardens. The Grimms said there were more stairs in the streets than in the houses.

A few days after we arrived we climbed up to a festival on the castle grounds in a forest just thick enough to mix some shade into the sunlight, with hundreds of market stalls filled with arts and crafts and fine foods, grilling sausages, frying crepes and kebabs. Long-tabled beer gardens were full of cheerful feasters. The Christmas markets are distinct but equal: mulled wine (Glühwein), roasted chestnuts, Lebkuchen and gingerbread, traditional wood-carvings, etc.

> *"Of course our lives are still mostly the daily round of work, chores, meals, TV; nothing special. But when we do go out the door, there's a wealth of the rich and strange."*

We had bad luck with cars. It's hard to find an automatic car in Europe so we spent a lot of time searching, then had to travel many miles to inspect them. We found a Honda Civic we called *Grünzwerg*, the Green Dwarf. We were surprised to learn one day that she needed a new "poem". Our trusty dictionary lifted the fog: "Dichtung" also means "gasket".

Austria

I suspected I was out of academia for good because I was taking a non-university position that might well be permanent. But it was liberating to discover that I could do something other than teach and research in my subfield. And in fact the search for a writing-editing job didn't take too long. As well, I was part of something valuable and exciting: medical devices that allowed the hearing-impaired to hear. Finally I had learned a healthy disgust for professorial posturing, arrogance and exploitation of junior colleagues who would toil long hours for years for practically nothing. When the new director said they work to live, not live to work, it was music to my ears. In Innsbruck we found a flat on the side of an Alp a block away from a cable car going up the Nordkette mountain chain one way (to ski slopes and the peak) and down to the middle of the city the other way. We had a small yard with a patio, a koi pond and views of the whole city and the silver-blue river Inn below, and the snow-capped, green-shouldered mountains all around. The place cannot take a bad picture. Our first time skiing again after 20 years, in what was effectively our back-yard, is one of those glorious memories. At end of day we sat on an edge of the slope with boots in the snow, glasses of *prosecco*, music playing and parasailers floating in the great blue spaces.

The Netherlands
Another fellowship came through after I thought it was all over. It was a pleasure to be back among the eggheads, writing and publishing, meeting and conferencing both near and far.

We moved to Amsterdam by overnight train (with our mover following) through the Alps, then on from Munich to emerge into 9 a.m. sunlight at Centraal Station, hectic but magnificent (designed by the Rijksmuseum architect), and the yet more hectic city centre. We went from the courtly to the dungeon-like: our residence at the southern edge of the city. But it was close to work, fine for a year and we saved some money.

Amsterdam's a small big city, they say, and we loved exploring by bike, tram and foot. I preferred to target neighbourhoods for a thorough wander. Best of all, you can rent small boats to cruise the canals. There's no better way to experience Amsterdam's unique architecture and boating culture. Nearby smaller towns are less crazy and more polished (Haarlem, the Hague, Alkmaar, Utrecht).

Our next move, a jump from A to B, Amsterdam to Bavaria, was a disaster. Beware cut-rate services sprouting like mushrooms, the downside of ICT. When our first truck left us in a last-minute lurch, we could hire only two smaller ones, both of which I had to accompany in our rental car (twice in two days!), the second time, through an alpine blizzard (in spring!) after midnight — around 24 hours driving all told. Of course, we arrived on April Fool's Day. But now we're semi-settled in Germany again, in reach of the mountains, Nuremberg, Munich and Prague.

Risks, losses, lessons, gains

We've learned much (about our occupations and expertises and the wider world) and done much. We've discovered new ways to speak, travel, work and live, as well as people from all places and walks of life.

Europe is fizzing with history, art and culture — we've toured museums and explored buildings and monuments till our feet, eyes and brains ached; the masterpieces stick with us still.

Scale is important. European cities have been built for people (and horses) to walk in, not for cars as often they are in North America. It feels safe almost everywhere, probably because of greater equality. There's no comparison to major North American cities where you can walk a block in the wrong direction from a wealthy downtown (as we have in Toronto, San Francisco, Philadelphia) and suddenly feel you're in a war zone with barbed wire, garbage and ruin, people radiating danger and despair. Areas that locals think are dodgy are tame in comparison. Yet it's also far less conservative and regulated than Canada. The relaxed and trusting attitudes seem more sane than the litigation-shyness that can make things drab. The cliff walks in Ireland had no railings and we signed no waivers for Amsterdam boat rentals.

Of course our lives are still mostly the daily round of work, chores, meals, TV; nothing special. But when we do go out the door, there's a wealth of the rich and strange. As mid-term expats, we have the luxury of exploring at leisure, soaking up the culture over time, attuning to the calendar rather than following a whistle-stop schedule, and waiting for and taking part in events as they arrive, minor and local as well as tourist-worthy.

There is an element of permanent vacation in that. We have lived on an Alp and on the North Sea. We visit new lands with the greatest of ease. It feels a bit hedonistic, which gives us twinges of guilt. But it's also practical (building up skills and experience) and a constant struggle. If we revel in the bragging rights we accumulate, we're earning them, and those we make jealous always have guestrooms with us.

Will we stay? We often think of moving back. We know that wouldn't be easy, but we'll do it if the need arises. I never quite believe people who say they have no regrets. The thing is to learn from them and out-weigh them with contentments. Weighed so, we want for nothing. Now this is part of who we are — we've mastered the arts of travel, of relocation, of sinking into new places and situations and flourishing there. We move a little faster than a moving world. At times this calls up Groucho Marx's classic, "Hooray for Captain Spaulding":

Hello, I must be going,
I cannot stay, I came to say, I must be going.
I'm glad I came, but just the same I must be going.
La La. ...
I'll stay a week or two,
I'll stay the summer thru,
But I am telling you,
I must be going.

But Walt Whitman gives us the other side of the same sentiment in "Song of the Open Road":

Afoot and light-hearted I take to the open road,
Healthy, free, the world before me,
The long brown path before me leading wherever I choose.
Henceforth I ask not good-fortune, I myself am good-fortune, ...
You road I enter upon and look around, I believe you are not all that is here,
I believe that much unseen is also here. ...

You but arrive at the city to which you were destin'd, you hardly settle yourself to satisfaction before you are call'd by an irresistible call to depart...

Michael Sinding
Age 45
Canada / Amsterdam / Erlangen, Germany

Mike Sinding is a wandering scholar of language and literature. He has published a book, Body of Vision: Northrop Frye and the Poetics of Mind *(2014), and many articles in scholarly journals. Melissa Sinding is a wandering jewelry-maker (Practical Magic Jewels).*

Mike's recommended Websites
   Ireland: movetoireland.com
   Germany: toytown.germany.com; marburg.de; marbuch-verlag.de
   Austria: innsbruck.info/en/home.html; innsbruck.com
   The Netherlands: iamsterdam.com; iamsterdam.com/en-GB/living/Expatcenter/about-the-expatcenter; lauraspeaksdutch.info

"Being exposed to the existence of other languages increases the perception that the world is populated by people who not only speak differently from oneself but whose cultures and philosophies are other than one's own."
— Dr. Maya Angelou

Dutch in Portugal

Wim Minten

Countryside Holland in the 50s was recovering from the impact of World War II with an attitude of "can do" and "let's get over it" by hard labour and a clear vision of a better and peaceful future for the children. Agriculture and some industry determined the social and physical landscape. The telephone was slowly going mainstream, the first black and white TV sets penetrated all levels of society and cars became more than just vehicles for notaries and doctors. Double glazing and central heating were not common yet, and hot water bottles and lots of blankets made freezing winter nights manageable.

Community life flourished because money became available due to increased production, religious ideas shifted and labour hours were reduced. Streets and houses needed to be built for the expanding population and increasing speed of life. Schools and TV programs taught general knowledge and abilities needed to earn a good living. Windows were traditionally huge and inviting in Holland to let in both sunlight and neighbours' views. Memory was a board game played over a cup of hot chocolate and biscuits on cold and windy winter nights.

My Story

It sounds idyllic and for sure it was peaceful, fun, inspiring and loving. Yet somehow I never fit in.

From early on I wondered "what am I doing here", with here referring not just to family and the country but the planet as well. A sense of not being in the right place ran through my thoughts.

Catholic dogma states that we have only one life, so the idea of reincarnation was not common and definitely not stimulated in that environment. Little did I know about other world views and religions. Time was spent learning the things the government regulated and school supplied.

It was not much of an effort to keep up with language and math. At primary school I ended up in the five best of my grade year after year. It just didn't keep me going, always wondering when the interesting stuff would come up. In fifth grade, English classes started. The world grew beyond the village square and German television programs. It felt completely natural to learn English, as if it involved no real effort. Consciousness however was still limited to being Dutch, son of so and so, village boy, age, gender, etc. The next city was a dangerous place and not within the scope of daily awareness.

High school changed the game a bit. I was not one of the few clever ones anymore. There were more newspapers to be read than the one at my parents' house and different cultures became fact rather than fiction. Someone pointed out the *I Ching* to me. It clicked and yet the daily struggle with languages, math and physics didn't allow delving deep into it. The boy and girl games my friends engaged in eluded me. Although born and raised in Holland, the normal adolescent interaction remained to me a mystery. Culturally I just could not get it. By means of family background, going out on the weekends involved drinking beer (lots of it) and then going after the girls, dancing a foxtrot half drunk and ending up kissing the girl of choice at the graveyard gate behind the church. Looking back it seems weird, but at that time it was the only reality I knew and by that virtue considered normal. The idea of dancing sober is a concept my brothers still have difficulty embracing.

After high school in 1976 I ended up in the office of a chain of retail stores. One year later my boss asked if I had studied English and math and upon confirmation, I was invited to the computer department. The mainframe had its own room with air-conditioning and a full-time technician who kept his beers hidden and cool in one of the tape units. My geek life took off then. With most family and friends into agriculture and construction, talks over a drink rarely included my professional activities and thus increased my feeling of "not being part of this".

A colleague invited me to go by car on a holiday to Greece. We embarked on the VW van turned into a camper followed by a Renault 5 and thought ourselves explorers and navigators. In a strange way sitting in the shade of an olive tree with a cup of coffee and later a beer whilst reading *Zen and the Art of Motorcycle Maintenance* felt much more natural than programming a mainframe in an old warehouse-turned-computer room. The book talked about parallel realities and spiritual aspects of normal everyday life and created my desire to "know more". Greek museums didn't speak much to me but the monastery on a mountaintop in Meteora did. (en.wikipedia.org/wiki/Meteora)

Sweet memories of past lives in peaceful contemplation emerged, seriously upsetting my adolescent desire to make a career, get a big car and a blond partner and earn buckets of money. Those four weeks were the most impressive holiday ever. Something clicked and a door opened to allow a trace of light in, never to be closed again. And yet there was a marriage and lots of IT courses to come before the old rusty hinges gave in enough to allow entrance to the other side of reality and let go of the "me, Dutch" fixed identity.

The next job was with an agricultural software house where we developed software for the management of intensive agriculture. Total chain control was emerging both in agriculture and in the awareness of the happy few who had read the book *Nineteen Eighty-Four* by George Orwell. It was scary to read the book and see (from that moment's state-of-the-art IT point of view) that everything described in the book was just a few decades away.

Seeing the reality of food production and the similarities of the faith of those animals and humans, things started to fall into place. At the next annual review I asked my boss if we were contributing to a better world. He looked puzzled and asked if I wanted a raise. No thanks, more of the same was not good enough anymore

The big shift

Nineteen eighty-eight was my year of change. I quit my job, ended a marriage, sold the house and started a search into the unknown; for the time being mainly within the safe borders of the Netherlands. Astrology, homeopathy, shiatsu, meditation and vegetarianism became my new Windows 3.11. Family and friends were buying their first desktop PCs and I was moving out of IT into unknown territory again, leaving them puzzled as to why I didn't engage more enthusiastically in discussions on the advantage of bigger hard disks or the latest version of Basic.

When I joined a daily meditation group in 1991, they all thought I had lost it. How right they were. Arriving in India at Delhi airport at 1 a.m. in a humid, hot and extremely polluted environment, I had tears rolling down my cheeks... "I am home, finally I am home".

It took a few visits to realize that home indeed is where the heart is, but that the home from past life memories has moved on as well.

India as a culture and vibration appealed to me, but the modern-day physical reality was a bit too much separated from my organized and clean Dutch origins.

So I spent some time in Oxford and Umbria to taste the differences Europe has to offer. Somewhere in between a request came to help out in Lisbon, Portugal, to rebuild a meditation centre. Gentle people and climate, good food and enough work made it a happy stay with the mix of old European, Indian and South American personalities adding to a global flavour.

Life went on and I returned to Holland, wondering ever more: "What am I doing here?"

Finally the right question emerged: "Where do I want to live?" The answer was Portugal. I sent an email to one of the ladies I had worked with and got a simple reply: "Just come".

That sounded too simple. So in another email I asked about housing, transport, jobs, income, etc. Again the reply: "Just come". Looking up I asked, "Are You trying to tell me something?"

Portugal

What to do. I sold my furniture and cancelled the rented apartment. Telling my parents I sold my bike made them realize it was for real. A Dutchman without a bike is like an American without wheels; hard to imagine. Lisbon airport was warm and inviting and my friend was waiting at the airport, ready to put the two suitcases in her car.

First she asked, "Where would you prefer to live, near the beach in a somewhat small apartment or near the airport in a bigger one?" Coming from a cold and wet country, the choice was fairly simple.

We entered the apartment and she gave me her spare car key and a mobile. "You keep the car and I will call you when I need it, so you can pick me up."

The fridge and table were full of food because "you don't know your way around and don't speak the language". Looking up I said, "Okay, Your way". It seemed too easy to be true. She bought me stuff and showed me around for the next three months. The sky opened up after years of financial and health issues.

Practicality

First things first. Living in Portugal requires a few basic things and a few profound things. The basics are about getting registered. Best place to go is the Loja de Cidadão in Lisbon or any of the other registered cities (citizens shop) which offer one-stop registration of most essentials. (portaldocidadao.pt/portal/pt/lojacidadao).

Take copies of your relevant documents and plenty of patience and time. Things have dramatically improved over the last 10 years but still, simple things can take hours to complete if they're not 100 percent according to the book — and the fact that you are reading this in English already implies that it is not fully according to the book. Most desks have at least one employee who speaks English, but don't count on it.

From memory, you need to go to SEF first to register the fact that you are going to stay in Portugal and do some background checks. Serviço de Estrangeiros e Fronteiras is located in Lisbon and various other places. It has an English website: sef.pt/portal/V10/EN/aspx/page.aspx.

When all is well and you have some documents to prove you are legally residing in Portugal, you can continue your journey.

Next stop would be the tax office to get a tax ID: aka Número de Indentificação Fiscal (NIF). The website of Angloinfo has great info on all things related to moving to Portugal: portugal.angloinfo.com/moving/residency/fiscal-number-nif.

With the NIF and a proof of residence (rental statement or utility bill in your name) you can open a Portuguese bank account.

Learning the Portuguese language and culture is another essential if you are planning to stay more than a few weeks. Language and culture is in fact a package deal. Speaking the language fluently without understanding the cultural implications of the phrases is a recipe for frustration and distress.

During a positive thinking course, a German student complained that the Portuguese are inefficient. On asking her what seemed easier, to change her attitude or that of 10 million people, she looked puzzled. Countries exist on the basis of collective habits considered worth having. If you can't adapt, you will find yourself surrounded exclusively by other expats in no time.

De University of Lisbon gives language courses to students of all ages. They have intensive courses during summertime and regular courses throughout the year with professional teachers: letras.ulisboa.pt/pt (their website is in Portuguese only, but most staff is bilingual). Some local governments give language courses for foreigners as well, some of them for free. Check with the city hall (Câmara Municipal).

One common misunderstanding needs some explaining without going into detail about daily life as an expat in Portugal.

The word "amanhã" translates as "tomorrow". But beware, amanhã has no fixed position in time, unlike "tomorrow", which generally applies to a moment in time within 24 hours from "now". Amanhã in fact means "not now" without any reference to a possible time in the future. It can drive you crazy in the beginning. "When can I come back to pick up the document, car, shopping, etc.?" Amanhã means, "I have no idea, but it's not ready yet and I can't guarantee that it will be ready in the near future". It sounds a bit extreme like this, but it has happened to me several times. On Monday I asked a painter when he planned to prime a door in order for a carpenter to finish it the next day. He said, "amanhã" So I thought, Tuesday the door will be painted, and the carpenter can do his job on Wednesday. No bad intentions on either side, just a very different cultural understanding of what really matters in life.

Once I needed a signature of a medic. I offered her the document to be signed but kept a firm grip on my side of it, smiling at her all the time whilst chatting along. First she said come back tomorrow (amanhã) but on insisting and maintaining my composure, she decided that it could be signed right away after all. After some time you will get the hang of it.

Why Portugal?

One morning in April in Holland I went for a bike ride and could not warm my hands afterward. It was not freezing, just some 12 degrees Celsius. Time to move to a warm country. Climate influences our mood and sense of belonging.

In a strange way the social interaction in Portugal makes so much more sense than the Northern European attitude. Every now and then I have to go back to the North to fully appreciate it, but it feels so normal deep down. Age doesn't matter that much, and there's respect and space for people's quirks and a gentleness in dealing with others. The directness of the North has its benefits and guarantees a financially comfortable life, but like the pin-up in an old *Playboy* magazine stated, "I would trade Southern comfort for Yankee know-how anytime."

You don't expect a Grand Old Lady to walk swiftly like a deer. It's clear that the golden age of Portugal is something hidden in the tiny cobblestone streets behind small arches or huge doors for carriages and horsemen. Lisbon breathes a glorious past that makes you look back in awe at what went on there a mere 200 years ago. Dolphins used to swim up to the Praça de Commercio in the middle of downtown, adding sweetness and magic to the stunning sunsets over the river.

Cultural depth and the beauty of design keep me here, and a lack of integrity and cleverness makes me long for "home" at the same time. Churches and fortresses close to 2,000 years old are physical reminders of all that has happened here and the vibrations of it somehow ended up in the soil and the sweetness of Algarve's oranges. The relationship with India is obvious in Martin Moniz and other parts of Lisbon, but at close observation also in the general attitude of the Portuguese. Portugal is in many ways still a port to the Orient and as such, she has much to discover.

Wim Minten
Age 59
The Netherlands / Lisbon, Portugal

Wim's website is on how to use modern technology in a healthy way: ehsfree.com.

An Expat Story – Moving to Morocco

Tristan Morton-Clark

My wife and I first laid eyes on each other 45 years ago in the markets of Marrakesh.

I was browsing the colours and smells of the markets when my eyes fell upon another young traveller. She didn't notice me at first but I watched her barter energetically for a carpet. I followed her for what seemed like an age before I got the courage to say hello. Forty-five years later the rest is wonderful history. We have travelled, laughed, cried and raised five beautiful children along the way; and through the many countries we explored we always knew our hearts lay in the warm sun of Morocco.

We had made a comfortable and loving home for ourselves and our children among the rolling hills of Cornwall but now with all five children grown, our lives were once again ours and our sights quickly returned to Morocco. However, after 40 years of living in Cornwall our roots had grown deep and it would not be easy to leave.

Over a period of years we went back and forth travelling Morocco in search of a place to retire. At times we were disheartened. Places that were once beautiful had lost their charm and were overrun with tourists and stores filled with tack. The Western world had reached the places we remembered dearly, but we didn't give up hope. Slowly we made a list of places where we could see ourselves spending our golden years, and after much consideration we found our dream house. I remember this point well, the ball rolling towards our final (though this may sound dramatic, for us, we were ready to accept it as thus) resting place was about to pick up some momentum. But we had a few key stages left before we could leave.

Getting the house was surprisingly easy and an all-around smooth operation. After years of careful budgeting, my wife and I had put together a reasonably nice nest egg on which we could live out our dream years together. Though to be honest our whole lives have been quite a pleasant dream.

When we were first together, my wife-to-be was working part time as a cleaner and living the simple life out of a caravan. Her ease with her own existence made her a pleasure to be around. For me, well, I was making my way in the world making and selling my own jams. Looking back and then comparing to today's world, it's a wonder children don't become overwhelmed with it all. The cost of living is madness. But then very few of us have it easy at all, so to complain in pointless indeed. Back to my career, I made and sold jams for a number of years living blissfully between my van and my girlfriend's caravan when by chance, and for the life of me I can't remember how, I was at a local fish market watching the morning's proceedings and quite captivated by the speed of it all and the friendly banter regarding the catch that morning and who was buying what. The rest of the tale is like so many others of how one seemingly small event leads on to the rest of your life story.

After the market had finished that morning, I spoke with some of the local merchants, made some friends and contacts in the industry, and with that my foot had been placed in a now-open door. Some months later I rented a small office and quickly I was on the market floor bidding for fish I could later sell to local restaurants. In the next 40 years I would see myself moving from small offices to larger ones, getting my own processing plant and a team of employees.

The year was now around 1978 and my wife-to-be and I were living in a nice country house with room to grow and while of course life threw up its challenges, my memories are all sweet ones.

Back to the story of Morocco. To get the house we wanted we had the option of finding an agent to do the work for us whilst we sat comfortably at home. Or we could go back to the country we loved, find the person selling the house and speak with them directly. I've always found that the easy option is a sure-fire way to avoid adventure so we packed our travel bags and got on the next plane to Morocco. In our many visits to the country we had made friends with a few of the locals, so this made finding the seller easier and we eventually found him. Though he was obviously pleased to meet us, he didn't speak any English, which of course made negotiations a bit tricky. But our friends in the area were willing to help us with translating.

Initially we sensed that our seller was a little uneasy selling the house to foreign invaders, but over a series of meetings he warmed to us and with minimal effort we negotiated a price that made everybody happy. I would recommend all persons to make every effort possible to deal without estate agents, though of course it takes more effort in some respects and one must take time to get any agreements in writing. Overall it was a pleasurable and a relatively stress-free experience. All in all the process took about two months, but by the end of it contracts were drawn and signed, money exchanged and we were the proud, very proud, owners of a home in Morocco. Things were moving along.

The next step for us was to organise visas, though at this stage we had put that process to the back of our minds. We thought in the worst-case scenario we could live out our time on a holiday visa occasionally leaving the country to renew our status. This was the fail-safe, fall-back option. As it happened, however, the process of getting a long-term visa for Morocco was relatively painless and straightforward. We started the proceedings by going to the Moroccan Embassy, which we combined with a trip to London. My wife suggested we try this after watching me struggle with the Internet approach of applying. I've always been more conformable with face-to-face methods of communication; for me, it's a much easier way to get information into my head.

It was my first time in an embassy of any kind so I was excited to see what went on inside these grand

and sometimes heavily guarded buildings. The excitement was short lived. Shortly after arriving at the embassy and having looked for a person to talk to, we were approached (obviously we looked clueless and lost) and told the waiting time to see an advisor was almost three hours. Well we'd come this far so we decided it was time to play the waiting game. It seemed that all of the embassy was off limits for wandering about and general sightseeing, so all we could do was sit. Luckily we had books, smart phones and the art of conversation, something we'd perfected over the years.

The time went by and we were eventually called. At this point I'd actually worked myself into a slight state of nervousness. What if we were denied access to the country? After all, we had just gone and bought a house. Perhaps the person interviewing us would find it all cocky? Perhaps they were having a bad day also. I didn't tell my wife my mind was in a bit of a negative spin but there was no going back now. We were already through the door. As it turned out, we were really quite fortunate. Upon walking through the door we were greeted with an exceptionally warm smile and asked to sit down. It's amazing how much a simple smile can do to ease a troubled mind.

After much conversation, both formal and informal, we all agreed it was a good idea for us to retire and live the rest of our lives in Morocco. The technical issues that needed sorting would be a series of fairly hefty forms that are too boring to go into here, but I can point out a few of the essential criteria that were needed in order to make ourselves eligible:

- Sufficient funds to sustain ourselves

- Knowledge of the local customs and general ways of life
- Language, we spoke some already but agreed to attend classes on arrival to the country

It's still a lucid dream looking back on the events that brought my wife and me to where we are now. About five months after our final interview, on Wednesday, August 13, 2013, an eagerly awaited letter fell through the door containing the words that we had waited so long to read — those that confirmed our eligibility to retire to Morocco, and also within the envelope were our passports containing our new visa status. Needless to say, we were delighted, over the moon, ecstatic and a whole bunch of other words that describe happiness.

Even now as I write this while looking out across the Moroccan countryside, I think back and all the events in my life that have led me to now seem like a dream. And as for the now part, well, living in Morocco has been better than expected and it sounds a little sad, but every now and then we give one another a little pinch just to make sure we're not dreaming.

Tristan Morton-Clark
Age 65
UK / Morocco

How in the Hell Did This Happen?

Jackie Gambill

As a military couple, my husband and I were lucky with our duty stations (among them, Naples, Italy; Key West, Florida; and Agana, Guam) and we thought we'd given the travel bug a pretty good run for its money before we left the service. Newly civilian, we launched careers, bought a home, raised our kids and pets, and acquired a lot of things.

Now comfortably middle class but still too young to retire, we started talking about *someday* traveling again. But when I was laid off and a new job wasn't on the immediate horizon, we considered our lack of constraints — we were renting, no pets, grown children, (so far) no grandchildren and we're in good health — and decided *why wait?*

It's as if the universe heard us ask the question, because in short order we happened across a Facebook post that led us to a long-term house-sitting opportunity in Belize, a locale that had figured in our travel dreams largely because English is its primary language.

If you haven't yet heard of house-sitting, it's a growing trend among travelers, especially baby boomers. Homeowners in, say, Canada, decide they'd rather be somewhere warm for the winter and advertise their property through a house-sitting platform or word of mouth. A house-sitter who may enjoy the cold weather (especially if it's for a limited amount of time) gets the opportunity to live there like a local, but rent-free. It's a win for both parties.

Our decision needed to be made quickly, and it was scary and exhilarating to consider. Do we stay within the safety net of our current lives, or do we leap and hope that a new, more flexible net will appear?

We leapt, and the next six weeks were a whirlwind of activity: From messages exchanged online we progressed to meeting the owners, then packing and cleaning our rental house and sorting, selling or stowing the bulk of our household goods.

We left for Belize with six stuffed suitcases between us; at the time it didn't seem like nearly enough to sustain us. Now, several months and three sits in, we've whittled to just four and it still seems like too much. I fully expect us to keep trimming until we have only what we need or really want with us.

Some people have asked us how it feels to be homeless; doesn't that bother us? We prefer to think of it as being *home-free*, and no, it doesn't bother us at all. It's liberating. It's interesting. And traveling like this is a fun way to see how others live and to see what we can and can't live without.

AT HOME ABROAD

Sometimes it's challenging — like when it takes two hours to do something that should take five minutes. Or when you have to go to six locations to find the one thing you want. Or because you are constantly converting mileage or currency or language in your head. Sometimes it's humbling — when you can't speak the language, as happened occasionally in Belize and often across the border into Mexico. Or when you see the size of the home where a young family of five lives without many of the conveniences we take for granted, and yet they are content — happier, in fact, than many folks we know.

Sometimes it's a little scary. You may as well get used to the wildlife because they're out there. Get used to thinking on your feet too because you'll often have to. And just accept that as a foreigner, you're often viewed as an easy mark.

We get asked a lot how we did it, and there really is no magic solution. Two things that will help are preparation and the willingness to let go of your comfort zone. There's a mental as well as physical process to this "letting go" — whether it's your possessions you're concerned about or not having control of the environment around you — so use the time that you pack and plan to educate yourself and calm your fears.

You may not need as much money as you think, but you do need some so a working plan to fund your travels is a necessity, even if those plans end up changing (and they probably will). If you don't have a trust fund (ha!) and will need cash flow as you travel, you may be able to work remotely. Just know what you're getting into: Does the area you want to visit have dependable Internet connectivity? And are foreigners allowed to work there? Even if the answer is yes, be sure you know the appropriate processes and regulations before you begin.

Make sure your travel documents are in order and that you understand whatever visa regulations are in place where you will be. For instance, in Belize we were required to visit Immigration every 30 days for a visa extension while we were there. In Honduras, we received an automatic 90-day visa upon arrival. You are responsible for knowing the rules and abiding by them, and you could be fined if you miss deadlines.

Facebook and Skype make communicating with family and friends easier, but it's also a good idea to have at least one person who knows your travel plans and can act on your behalf while you are away, preferably through a power of attorney. You can enroll with the Smart Traveler Enrollment Program, a tool of the US government to relay information that may be critical in an emergency. And don't forget to keep your info current on the STEP website as you move about.

Realize that you may have to do without some conveniences you're used to. We really appreciate what we've left behind — all those things we took for granted in our modern lives. For example, in one off-the-grid sit, we learned the hard way how to manage our power and water usage and did without on both counts as we learned from our mistakes. Less importantly, we sometimes miss our own bed linens or a specific food that's not available where we are.

But these inconveniences are almost always made up for with what *is* available where we are: a borrowed home that's usually more than adequate for our needs and often much more than that; new and sometimes unusual food; and experiences we could never have at home, like the day we found a baby toucan in the tree just outside our home-for-the-moment. And the day we spent exploring a thousand-foot waterfall, relaxing in refreshing plunge pools and exploring a huge cave. What else have we gained? A real awareness of resources and the environment, and how much can be wasted through inefficient energy and water use. We have a ton of empathy for anyone attempting to speak our language, however badly they may go about it. Maybe most importantly, we're less stressed and more content than we've been in many years.

If you use your common sense, trust your intuition, and aren't afraid to look like an idiot now and then, you can thrive as an expat. Have fun out there!

Jackie Gambill
Age 55
US / Belize / Florida, US

Ray and Jackie Gambill are a longtime American couple (34 years) who met in Naples, Italy, and have lived many places around the world since. Not quite ready to retire, they jumped at the chance to house-sit at several locations in Central America last year and had the time of their lives. They're currently back in the States, going to school, paying bills and plotting their next move.

"Americans who travel abroad for the first time are often shocked to discover that, despite all the progress that has been made in the last 30 years, many foreign people still speak in foreign languages."
— Dave Barry

From Oaxaca to LA

Soraya Heydari

My story is somewhat anomalous amongst my age group in Britain. Extended travel abroad is an activity reserved for the privileged in their gap year, for them to demonstrate 'practical skills' on their CVs to potential employers and their adventurous nature to friends back home on their Facebook feed. Certainly not because their chosen profession barely affords them a decent standard of living at home, like me.

My decision to bail was triggered by a series of events that began with a misguided decision to attend a useless university for a useless degree in a lonely, expensive town. Over the course of the year, I found my mental health deteriorating at a rate identical to my grades until both could go no lower and I stayed awake for days, hardly making sense to my concerned housemates, hardly eating. The very idea of creating a social life or attending lectures became laughably impossible. I remember looking in the mirror of the messy shared bathroom one day and gasping at the pale, drawn face that stared back. Lack of sunlight had turned my skin papery and yellow and peppered my cheeks with acne, which contrasted horribly with the purple circles around my eyes. I barely recognized myself and knew that something had to give. Within the week, I'd given away nearly all my stuff, found a job as a nanny in China and booked the tickets.

While in Asia, I met and fell for a writer from Nevada, and after my job ended I flew to join him in Vegas. Incredibly, Las Vegas turned out to be an environment much harsher and more unforgiving than urban China, and the struggle to preserve my mental health began all over again. By this time I had become a published writer and my partner was still working on his novel, the same one he'd been working on for the last decade, supposedly his magnum opus. Day after day we sat at either end of our rickety breakfast table in our studio apartment, typing furiously and trying to ignore the drunken arguments on the other sides of both walls and sirens that cracked through the air.

A big blow was dealt when my partner lost a long-term gig; and when we totted up the numbers, we knew that even little luxuries we enjoyed would soon be gone. As well as this my visa was running out, and I couldn't face a return to England. So we looked closer.

During his misspent youth, my partner had supposedly made his way south of the border with a group of college friends, mostly under the influence of psychedelic mushrooms, and ended up finding his enlightenment beside some ancient ruins in the state of Oaxaca. He recounted stories of plentiful, delicious food, wonderful people and most importantly (to me) a wonderfully cheap lifestyle. I began to get the old, familiar tingle of excitement I feel at the thought of going somewhere new as I Googled pictures of Oaxaca and read accounts from other travelers. Before we could overthink things, we had booked our flights to Mexico City and organised the six-hour bus ride to what we hoped was the centre of Oaxaca. We stuffed our dirty clothes into a couple of old backpacks and hitched a ride to the airport.

I stepped off the bus in Oaxaca with my boyfriend, felt in my pocket for my bankcard and realized it had been stolen. Resigned, I called my father from an Internet café to wire some money and prayed that this would be the end of our bad luck. But it wasn't. My boyfriend had screwed up our hotel booking, and exhausted and penniless we slumped down on our luggage and fell asleep in the bus station.

The money arrived and we booked ourselves into a local hostel the next morning and looked for a place to live. The Mexico I'd visited as a teenager with my parents had been the Disneyland, AK47-guarded Americanized ghetto of Cancun, so the real Mexico was something of a culture shock. Pickup trucks with far too many teenagers crouched in the back and beat-up old sedans rumbled through the cobbled streets, pumping out polka music and black exhaust fumes while tiny abuelas sold pots of mangoes from their carts and crowds of locals and the odd tourist milled around, talking animatedly. The streets were striking, with even the oldest, crumbliest buildings adorned with a decorative touch and bright, cheerful colors. The architecture was a mix of native stucco and colonial buildings and the grandeur was juxtaposed with the angry political slogans and sardonic cartoons spray-painted across them — the angry, raw cracks in Oaxaca's perfect façade.

A few days after we arrived, I browsed Craigslist and came across an ad for a dog-sitter in El Centro. I arranged a meeting with Annie, a graduate student who gave us a run-down of the job and tour of their beautiful, lofty apartment.

Opposite the mayor's house, their conspicuously red-bricked building had once been a European embassy but now housed a handful of Oaxacans and expats. At the center was a beautiful courtyard, filled with all manner of beautiful plants and flowers in pots and hanging baskets. I quickly made friends with her four boisterous little dogs. We mentioned we were looking for a permanent place to live and Annie called down in Spanish to her landlady, who announced she had a place right next door around the time Annie would be coming back to Oaxaca from the US. Rent was to be a mere $400 a month — where else in the world could a writer in her 20s find that?

A few days later Annie and her roommate left and we settled into life. The space and the climate were gorgeous but as you would expect in a poorer country, there were sacrifices. Tap water was strictly off limits until it had been brought to a furious boil and the archaic irrigation system in Oaxaca meant the cracked, old pipes leaked in dirt from the ground. More than once I ran squealing from the shower at the slew of brown liquid streaming from the tap. Every Wednesday the 'agua man' would come and fill up our water supply, lugging gallons up the rickety old steps while I looked on guiltily and tried to tip him handsomely for his trouble. Mosquitoes were to be expected and I soon learned to tolerate a roach here and there, but the first time a confused scorpion made its way in I felt a pang of revulsion and homesickness. I made friends with other expats, mostly interesting retirees or old hippies and backpackers, and met the local kids in the punk and metal music scene. I went to their gigs in abandoned warehouses in the outskirts of town and experienced the local politics and unrest through their musical expression.

Oaxaca had a lot to offer. It's famous for its enormous, semi-outdoor markets selling incredible produce, which made cooking a lot of fun. But with the exchange rate, the price of eating out for two every other night was perfectly doable so we indulged. Curiously, the city has a large population of Italian settlers, which means it has an abundance of authentic Italian restaurants to choose from, as well as Moroccan, Indian and Chinese.

I settled into my new life, but things with my partner were becoming strained. I discovered lies in his past and found his refusal to behave sensibly baffling. Everyone had warned us not to drink iced beverages, as ice is often made with the filthy tap water but he didn't listen, starting every day with a delicious Oaxacan iced coffee. A doctor confirmed he had contracted dysentery. Annie's partner came back and we moved next door, growing more and more distant by the day, and I began to feel the deep ache of homesickness. That was when my mother visited. She saw how unhappy I'd become with my boyfriend, who truth be told had become abusive at this point, and as we ate breakfast at her hotel, she looked deep into my eyes and told me to ask myself if I was okay with this life.

After she left, Annie returned briefly. She'd actually been in Los Angeles sorting out her own apartment and offered me a lifeline in the form of an airbed downtown. I told her I would think, which I did, all the way down to Guatemala on a plethora of unsafe vehicles to renew my dwindling Mexican visa. When I returned, I told my boyfriend I wasn't happy with his drinking and he assaulted me. Literally alone, I packed my bags and left for the first plane to LAX. A friend I'd hosted a few years before who had luckily moved to LA picked me up and dropped me at Annie's.

A lot happened in the next three months, but notably I gained back the 20 pounds and the confidence I'd lost and met someone incredible. So incredible I felt like I'd made him up, not least of all when he picked me up for our first date and took me to see a band who'd been my favorite since I was 15. We've made a go of things and a year later we live in this incredible melting pot of a city and aren't planning on going anywhere soon. He makes music. I still write. We both surf, and I finally feel at home.

Soraya Heydari
Age 24
England / Oaxaca, Mexico / Los Angeles

Soraya is an Anglo-Iranian freelance artist, writer and blogger for the Huffington Post. *After traveling the world, she settled in Los Angeles where she surfs, cooks and lives. Take a look at what she's up to these days at* sorayaheydari.com.

The Main Reason I'm Here: Freedom to Be As I Am

Susan Schenck

Ultimately, it was Cuenca that broke up my 18-year marriage.

After a year and a half here, my husband Allen (who had never lived outside of California) couldn't take the cultural differences and altitude sickness any more. He despised the class system here (which is less subtle than the one in the US). On top of that, our issues came bubbling to the surface. He went back to the states in December 2011.

A year after our separation, I went back to him in San Diego to see if I could fetch him back to Cuenca.

He stretched out his arms as we viewed the breathtaking beach of Del Mar, California — no doubt one of the most beautiful beaches in the world. "Isn't *this* paradise?" he gushed. "You've got the beaches, the mountains, the desert, and the canyons. You don't have to worry about falling into a pothole, getting hit by a car when crossing the street, or getting electrocuted by a fence. Driving and walking are safe. The air is clean. You can find all the health supplements here."

Then came my unwavering retort: "But what price do you pay for these conveniences? I would have to sacrifice 40 hours of my life every week, *every year till I die*, just to supplement my meager pension. I would have to sell my soul just to put gas in the car to get to that job. Precious moments would be lost just to put salt and pepper on the table. And all for about 10 to 20 bucks an hour since the jobs I qualify for aren't here.

"I would be a slave whereas in Cuenca, *I am a slave set free*! I wake up every morning when I want to. I haven't used an alarm clock in years (except to catch an early flight or hit the organic markets). The hardest part of my day is making the bed. After two and a half years, *I am still in awe* that I get to spend the first five hours of every day in meditation, contemplation, devotional reading, listening to soothing music while I write and market my books online, and doing whatever my heart feels like. Then I run errands by walking, I exercise, and in the evenings I hang out with my friends.

"I have more friends after two and a half years in Cuenca than I had in 23 years of living in California. Most of the expats here are free. They own their own time. They have *free time* — the most valuable asset, especially as we grow older. We all have time to socialize and exercise and express our creativity.

"My health is better than ever because I have time to do yoga every day, work out at the gym a few times a week, and walk every day for an hour or two. My weight is what it was at high school, 120 to 125 pounds (I am 5'4"). I can afford (time and money-wise) to take dance classes and follow my passions. "If I came back to the states, I'd have to work. Then, just like all those years, I'd be too tired to spend much time with you, anyway. Maybe one quality hour a day. I love you. But I don't love any man enough to be a slave. I've had it with the system that for decades has consumed my life force.

"I'm going back to Cuenca. I'm going back *home*."

"It's a deal breaker," said my husband. "San Diego is my Aranachula (the home to the famous sage Ramana Maharshi, who refused to leave). Goodbye."

Remaining friends, we agreed to go our separate ways. My case is not unique. I know of other couples who parted due to the enchantment of Cuenca. But I also know others who compromised. One friend of mine came here because of her husband. But as soon as he suddenly died, she got to work selling their property so she could head back to the US. She hated it here so much that she swears she'll never remarry. "I will never defer to a man again."

Meantime, I love my life here so much that I've written a couple of books about it: *Expats in Cuenca: The Magic & the Madness* and *The Quilotoa Loop: Ecuador's Hidden Treasure*. I hiked the dangerous narrow rim of the Quilotoa Crater Lake, probably the most beautiful sight in Ecuador — one of those sights that makes you gasp in awe (such as Niagara Falls and the Grand Canyon).

There are four ecosystems in Ecuador (the Pacific Ocean beach, the Andean mountains, the Amazon jungle, and the Galapagos Islands), even though the country is only the size of Nevada. So there is *plenty* to see and do. Once you hit 65, transportation costs are 50 percent off (including local buses).

The climate here is ideal. In Cuenca, 8,000 feet up, you get the four seasons in one day: early morning is spring, afternoon is summer, early evening is fall, and late evening is winter. Some don't like the cloudy overcast which is frequent: many expats prefer a sunnier valley such as Paute or Vilcabamba.

The cost of living is perfect. I know people living on $800 a month, or even less. It just depends on how much you want to eat out and travel. But you can get an apartment here as low as $200, even less if you share a house with friends. Food is as little as $100 a month. (As an example, I'd pay a couple of bucks in California for a mango or avocado, whereas here they are three for a dollar!) Yoga classes are $5 a session. Buses are a quarter, and a cab will get you most anywhere for $3 or less.

People who come here often lose weight from all the walking. Cuenca is really a "walking city" with everything close and great sidewalks. Parks are abundant and even have what I call "adult playground equipment" — exercise equipment to help keep people in shape!

There is plenty of culture: free symphonies (which my friend in Chicago paid $25 for!), local rock 'n' roll bands, festivities, parades, old churches, museums and much more.

Most Americans who come here to check it out stay. Nonetheless, statistics show that 50 percent of expats return to their native country within five years. I've been here four and a half and as far as I can see, there's no turning back!

Susan Schenck
Age 59
San Diego, CA / Cuenca, Ecuador

Susan is the author of several books, including Expats in Cuenca: The Magic & The Madness *and* The Quilotoa Loop: Ecuador's Hidden Treasure. *She also gives raw food classes and health/weight-loss coaching. She can be contacted at* LiveFoodFactor@yahoo.com.

"One's destination is never a place, but a new way of seeing things."
— Henry Miller

Medellín

Ryan Hiraki

One day melts into another in Medellín. It is not a small city, but it is not a large one either. The people here say it is a big town. I suppose it is. It is a paradoxical place in a lot of ways.

Life moves slowly, mostly, but every now and then people are in a hurry and not always for the right reasons.

New restaurants open every month, serving different ethnic foods, even though the people here are so traditional that a lot of them have never had sushi.

There are countless opportunities for entrepreneurs, yet doing business can be difficult despite the lack of bureaucratic red tape.

The expat community grows every month, and you would think everyone would be supportive of each other's ambitions, but people are people and they seem to follow an old political adage from the United States: Your opponents are in the other party but your enemies are in your own.

Living here, quite frankly, is an adventure and that's why I like it.

The Vacation That Changed My Life

My road to Medellín had more twists and turns than San Francisco's Lombard Street.

I grew up in Hawaii in a town called Hilo, a place in which I thought I would live forever. It wasn't until I turned 18 that I started thinking about leaving to study on the "mainland," and in 1998 I finally left for the University of Nevada.

When I graduated in 2001, all I wanted to be was a journalist — someday a national correspondent for the *New York Times* — to see more of the United States, to record the country's biggest stories. Never once did I think about going abroad but I was young and naïve.

I remained that way for the first five years of my career until a few friendships changed everything.

In 2005 the midsize Florida newspaper where I worked hired a photographer who was born in India, raised in Germany, and educated at the University of Texas. He was aloof, like I can be, and talented, which I am not sure I am, but we got along from the beginning and became good friends.

The following year he decided he wanted to go to grad school, but before he started he would return to Germany for the summer. The World Cup would take place there.

He invited me to go and because I had never been to Europe, I thought, "What the hell, let's do it." It was such a great experience running into people from around the globe that I knew I wanted to see more of the world, to make at least one trip out of the states each year.

In 2007 I was determined to see a new continent, South America, and I was trying to decide between Brazil and Perú.

"What about Colombia?" a friend of mine said. His father is from a pueblo near Bogotá, and he had recently traveled to Cartagena for vacation. After he showed me the pictures from his trip, I was sold. I found a cheap plane ticket out of Miami and a great deal at an all-inclusive resort, and I was on my way.

I never imagined, never dared to consider, that I would someday make a home outside the United States.

The Risk

The tourism department of the Colombian government created a catchy slogan to market the country as an emerging tourist destination: "The only risk is wanting to stay."

The marketing minds had yet to develop it when I first landed, but I would become living proof, or at least anecdotal evidence, that the saying has merit.

I enjoyed the warmth of the Colombian people during that week in Cartagena as well as the historical sites, beautiful architecture and relaxing afternoons on the beach. I wasn't ready to stay but I knew I wanted to return.

Fast forward four years later to the eve of my graduation at the George Washington University, and I was on my way back to Colombia, this time to Medellín.

Following my trip to Cartagena I started reading more about the country, mostly about a place they called *La Ciudad de la Eterna Primavera,* The City of Eternal Spring.

I knew some of the history, the dark days of Pablo Escobar and the chaos that raged during the days of his drug cartel, but I began reading about a renaissance and I wanted to see it up close.

At the time I was writing about growth and development in Florida so I was intrigued how a Latin American city was transforming itself from the murder capital of the world into a hub of innovation and economic opportunity.

My vacation lasted a week but I knew after two days that I would be back.

The Fleeting Apple

My plan during my last months of grad school was to find a job in New York, something in public relations, which is what I studied for my master's degree. It wouldn't be the *New York Times,* my original dream, but I'd still be in the big city and that's what I wanted most.

I used to make one or two trips a year there, starting in the new millennium, and I knew I would love living there. The problem is that it's expensive. I would need a good job and the economy there, like so many other places, was a mess.

I sent out hundreds of resumes, many for jobs I could do easily, and the only interest I got was from companies that could pay me only a fraction of what I would need to live comfortably in what I believed was the greatest city in the world.

My trip to Medellín made me rethink things.

If I moved to Medellín, I could learn Spanish, something I had always wanted to do, and I had enough money saved to live there comfortably for about a year. Maybe I would find a job before I ran out of money. What the hell, let's do it, I decided. For the first time in my life, I would live outside the United States.

Three Months, Then We'll See

The line at Fort Lauderdale International Airport was moving slowly and I was beginning to second-guess myself. Was I making the right decision? Would I find a job? Could I fit in? What about the culture shock?

"Are you moving there?" the woman at the counter asked me when I gave her two suitcases to check in.

"Yes," I said, and I didn't say it with confidence. "I am."

She shook her head like I was crazy, but it was too late to turn back now. I am happy I didn't. I could survive three months, I decided, and we would go from there.

The people were friendly, that I already knew, so that made the transition easier. So did living with a bunch of expats.

Within a month, I had a job.

I had met David Lee, the editor in chief of *Medellin Living*, during my vacation there and in October 2011 he sent me an email and asked me if I wanted to help him develop his travel blog.

I had written one story for him about the Art Hotel, the place I stayed during my vacation, and another about my observations of the city. Now I would be writing a lot more.

When December came around, I headed back to the states for Christmas at my brother's house but I knew I would return to Medellín. Only one thing would need to change: my living situation, mainly because I wasn't learning Spanish living with people who always spoke English. For the first four months of 2012 I lived with a local family. I began to get curious about other countries in South America, if I would like any of them better than Colombia, and when I found a roundtrip ticket to Buenos Aires for just over $500, I bought it. In May I would make a new adventure.

Missing Medellín

I was gone two months and went to four countries — Argentina, Chile, Paraguay, Uruguay — and saw many great things. Among them were: the giant waterfalls at Iguazú, the Jesuit ruins just outside Encarnación, the beautiful architecture in Colonia del Sacramento, the history in Montevideo, the bodegas just outside Mendoza, and the top of Volcan Villarica in Pucón.

But I wanted to get back to Medellín. I missed home.

I had continued with my job with the *Medellin Living* blog while I was gone and looked forward to doing more when I got back.

I found other jobs as well: managing a hostel during the nighttime hours, then SEO writing and social media at a big Colombian company, and finally opening a tourism company. I learned a lot.

"Stumbling From Failure to Failure"

Culture shock doesn't apply in Medellín until you work for a Colombian company or start your own.

I am not trying to bash anybody, just to point out that they do business differently here than a lot of places and not just the United States but Canada and countries in Asia and Europe as well.

I liked the hostel job but left it for the job with the big company, which I left after a genuine case of miscommunication.

I began to explore another opportunity: opening a tourism company with one of the first friends I had made upon moving to Medellín, a guy who was born in Colombia but grew up in Miami.

Little did I know about his business ethics — they were terrible.

He robbed our company but worse, our clients. He even tried to intimidate me and one client by telling stories about how his father used to work for Pablo Escobar, something I have since found is probably not true, just another part of his con.

It is sad because I have met good people here. My ex-business partner doesn't realize how his duplicity hurts the image of his entire country.

I have moved on. As Winston Churchill says, "Success is stumbling from failure to failure with no loss of enthusiasm."

I always smile when I read that.

Redemption

When Alvaro Uribe was Colombia's president, he put in place a handful of laws to make foreign investment easier in his country. He knows it is essential for growth. His policies have made it easy for people to start their own businesses, something I have decided to do myself. No partner this time.

My Spanish is pretty good so I can do everything when it comes to sorting official paperwork. That was my only obstacle at one time.

I am based in Bogotá, focused on online media, including a return to real journalism, writing for a fast-growing online magazine called *Ozy*. I am working with a Florida consulting firm as well, mainly writing grants and editing video for its clients, a handful of nonprofit organizations.

I like being on my own. If I fail, there is no one to blame but myself. I can live with that.

Crowds and Questions

I finally made it to Perú.

It was seven years after I first thought about going, but I did it. The trip included a trek to Machu Picchu, naturally. We got there as dawn flooded the valley, giving the ruins a special glow, a delicate sheen.

My Colombian friend, Sebastian, and I spent the entire morning there, a good six hours, before we walked down the hill and back to the hostel to shower, change and go to lunch. We had hired a guide and seen almost every inch of the ruins and learned all about their history.

I was surprised by how many people were there, even during the early morning hours. I knew Machu Picchu was popular but I had no idea the crowds were already big by 6 a.m.

Most of the people were likely traveling for a bit and then would return to their home countries, to somewhere familiar. Others might find a home in Perú or another country where they had never lived before.

I wondered, for a moment, which ones would stay away from home, what kind of adventure they would have, where they would go, why they would make the trip. They would enjoy it, I thought to myself. Then I turned toward one of the many paths among the ruins and kept on moving.

Ryan Hiraki
Age 36
Hawaii, US / Bogotá, Colombia

Ryan is a foreign correspondent based in Latin America. He learned to speak Spanish in Colombia and has since been to Cuba, Mexico and most of South America. In his free time he loves cooking, cycling and reading. Follow him on Twitter at @ryantravelin.

"We live in a wonderful world that is full of beauty, charm and adventure. There is no end to the adventures we can have if only we seek them with our eyes open."
— Jawaharial Nehru

Intentionality with Flexibility: Weaving Our Lives in Another Culture

Susan and Richard Neulist

L iving intentionally has always been a part of my life and our lives together. I have thought often about the connection between living intentionally and having flexibility. Just like my yoga practice — it takes discipline and intentionality to build more flexibility.

This is how we have lived over the last five years since retiring from our jobs in *el Norte*. Both of us grew up in the northeastern US, and often our work was consulting during only part of the year. So we have always had time to satisfy the travel bug, and having no children has enabled us to live intentionally with flexibility. We have similar values so an alternative lifestyle never seemed like a challenge too difficult to undertake.

I never felt that we had an actual plan for this life-style other than "Let's try one year of living in Mexico and see how it goes." Our plan was to return to San Miguel de Allende (SMA), which we had previously visited, starting with a two-month house trade with a friend in SMA who wanted to be in North Carolina. We rented out our house in North Carolina for that first trial year and have every year since. We returned to SMA and we house sat with plans to rent after that. Then, as I have often said, this house-sitting lifestyle took on a life of its own.

Now, almost five years later we have had wonderful opportunities for eight to 10 months a year allowing us further travel in Spanish-speaking countries the rest of the time. The house-sitting experience, though not in the original plan, has enabled us to save $8,000–$10,000 a year, which we use for additional travel. Now we are booked a year in advance with requests for two or three years from now. Our vagabond ways make it impossible for us to plan several years out but having a plan for a year works.

We decided a long time ago that if we chose to live away from our family for extended periods of time, we would make sure to visit friends and family once or twice a year, and we have done so for all these years. It allows us to know that we are connected as always and of course technology makes this even easier.

Part of Richard's plan was to follow his inner voice toward a Latin culture in order to re-inherit his childhood experiences, as his mother was born in Guatemala. He believed this would bring him an insurmountable amount of joy and connect him to her Latina spirit, and it has. I had no connections to the Hispanic world but have embraced it as well. In our travels we have been able to reinvent ourselves without losing sight of our gifts and skills.

What is it like to live in another culture? We have always enjoyed adventures but I never thought about what it would mean to live in another country. At first I thought only about initially taking risks to do things differently. Living in Mexico seemed to be a wonderful way to get out of our routine and experience something new. What we found was much more than we could have imagined. A new language, new friends who speak it, vibrancy of living, trying on new pastimes and opening doors to volunteer experiences. Our lives have been richer since moving from our home country. Now we would find it hard to decide what that home country would be as "home" has become the place we are in at the moment.

One of the great "adventures" of our house-sitting lifestyle is that each month or so we have a new home, new neighborhood, new *ayudantes* (helpers), and new beautiful gardens and surroundings. It takes a certain amount of planning and executing a move each month; it requires us to pare down our belongings and collect, pack and move. To many this may seem overwhelming, but for us, it is now down to a science. Two hours in one house packing, two hours in another unpacking — simple and doable and the price is right.

We use the savings from our living expenses for our adventure travels to other countries or back to US for visits. This lifestyle has also helped me understand and be more accepting of myself. We decided in the beginning that we can never have more belongings than will fit into one taxi (along with ourselves). We have kept to this plan but I used to be hard on myself about having too much stuff — too many clothes, accessories, art supplies, etc.

As time has gone by, I've allowed myself the luxury of having more than I need as part of my identity. I enjoy nice clothing and we have a wonderful Tuesday Market with bargains galore. It is hard to pass up $100 items for $2–$5! So now I just remind myself that it is only a few hours in each home and then we are moving again for another month. We have a small storage space for the months when we are not in town and still fit into a cab when moving.

When Richard travels in a foreign country, he gets to view another culture which allows him to have a better sense of his own and to better understand the world as a whole — in effect, it gives him a third eye. What has changed most for us is that we find ourselves in a world without borders. Because of our abilities and resources, we are able to travel almost fluidly as if the world has no borders.

What are the benefits of this expat lifestyle?

For Richard one of the benefits is that we can live a bigger life while using less of our retirement resources. Other benefits are language and volunteer work — to be able to learn and communicate in another language, share life experiences, use the many skills acquired during our working lives and develop new ones.

For me the benefits are many but specifically communicating in another language. Originally I planned to rely on Richard for my Spanish communication but

I realized that if I really want to be part of another culture and have friends who do not speak English, I would have to learn Spanish.

I attended Warren Hardy Spanish School here in SMA for their four levels of programming and then we headed to Cuenca, Ecuador, for an immersion experience — living with a family and going to *Fundacion Amauta*. We even lived with different families so I would not rely on Richard to speak for me.

It was a wonderful experience. We lived only blocks from each other and met each morning on the bridge crossing the river between us. My "mama" Yolanda (who was younger than I) watched from her balcony window and enjoyed the "lovers" meeting every morning to walk to school. Richard came to our house many afternoons and "slept over" on the weekends. Now Yolanda and her family are *our* family and we have visited Cuenca several times since the first immersion.

The ability to walk and not need a car for transportation is another important benefit as it allows us daily exercise and is good for the environment. We know we never want to live long term in a place where a car is the only means of transportation.Having year-round fresh fruits and vegetables without shopping in giant grocery stores is a big plus for our vegan/vegetarian lifestyle.

How have we changed as people?

Mainly I feel younger because I feel more alive in this lifestyle. I plan each year basing my intentions on my values. Living in Mexico has allowed me to try new things and decide if I want to keep them as part of my life.

Examples include: tap dancing (I had this on a list when I did "The Artist's Way" over 20 years ago). So I bought tap shoes and went to class. I enjoyed it and will do it again when classes are available, but I realized it is not my real passion.

I attended an online Sketchbook Skool, have taken two courses, and intend to keep it up as I am enjoying drawing, painting and writing. It is something I can do creatively anywhere, especially while traveling.

I have tried acting (did not like the memorizing) and improv (more fun because there is no memorizing). Improv is related to my value of living in the moment and has been a wonderful way to "get out of myself," listen and be present. I do hope to continue with this. I have taken art classes and many yoga classes. I have given myself a yearly challenge in yoga and this has helped me move forward in my practice.

I like to look at my life as I look at my yoga practice — it takes discipline and planning and intention but needs flexibility in how it is accomplished. I hope to continue being intentional with flexibility.

Challenging myself in this new lifestyle has helped me to be more accepting as a person and as I grow individually, our relationship grows as well. What works well for us is that we support each other for our individual goals and dreams and at the same time we support our activities as partners and with friends who have enriched our lives tremendously.

Richard feels changed by having less stress and learning to seek out more people he enjoys being with (as many are retired), and he has come to accept more easily all people as equals. He is more aware of his convictions, and those convictions are deeper. He discovered his love of teaching and spending time with young people. He has developed his own style of teaching that goes with his personality and makes it totally fun for him.

Anything missing in this lifestyle?

I think we both miss the same thing — family. We speak to many on the telephone and of course with technology and social networking, we see our extended family and friends from all over the world. But this does not take the place of sitting in someone's kitchen with a cup of tea and just being together.

I must say that unless one lives as the Latin Americans do, with everyone under one roof or in the same town or vicinity, then it does not really matter where one is. When we lived in North Carolina, we did not have any family nearby and probably saw them as often as we do now. So in writing, I realize this is not really a geographical issue but another example of intentionality to stay connected.

Susan and Richard Neulist
Ages 69 and 60
US / San Miguel de Allende, Mexico

Travel blog: mexicotravel-susan-ricardo.blogspot.mx
Vegan Food Adventures: vegan-food-adventures.blogspot.mx

"The loneliness of the expatriate is of an odd
and complicated kind, for it is inseparable
from the feeling of being free,
of having escaped."
— Adam Gopnik

Living in Costa Rica

Judith Donovan

Go confidently in the direction of your dreams. Live the life you have imagined. —*Henry David Thoreau*

Lightning flashes, thunder shakes and howler monkeys growl as the rain drenches everything in a sheet of impenetrable fog. My heart opens in gratitude. The cracked, dry earth, empty river beds, hungry cattle and our well have been crying, *We need rain*. Tomorrow when we navigate the gully-devastated roads, we will remember, *We need rain*. Our first contradiction of Costa Rica — wanting rain, then having to endure the undesirable results — seeps through.

As I sink into the luxury of an afternoon nap, warm breezes soothe my mind, the monsoon rain drowns all worries. Oops, the couch and I are getting wet! I jump up, close windows. I am at home in Costa Rica. Surrounded, penetrated by nature. I am at home amidst nature as few other civilized countries allow, at an affordable price near the ocean.

Once I told my son my dream was a yellow house by the ocean. Now I sit in that house! It is named Casa Amigos as we want to share the treasure of this land and share a dream I never thought possible, especially in a different country.

We are entering our fourth week in our new home base. Over the past few years we have increased our time here until it is our only official home. Despite struggles with the Internet, broken lights, hornets' nests and balky fans, we are relaxing in the glorious gift of rainy days.

A few months ago we shipped some necessary "stuff" from the states. As we were adjusting to our new home, one day a huge frog jumped out of the upstairs toilet. Next day I got up at 3 a.m. to a multitude of tiny frogs in the downstairs toilet! Later that day when I turned on the water to take a shower, again I screamed. Medium-sized frogs came pouring out of the faucet. Like Goldilocks I yearn to accept this place as just right, the middle way.

Now we are alternating from days of marveling at the welcoming people, the lushness of warm rain, and profuse textures of greens to days of frustration and discouragement at nonfunctioning basics like the Internet, international calling, setting up bank accounts and dealing with language barriers.

What a challenge to remain calm in this beautiful environment. My usual way of meditation does not fully hold me with all these new experiences. I think of the Tibetan sand mandala. The monks spend day after day painstakingly constructing them with minute, varied colored crystals of sand. The precise details evolve slowly, intricately with all the colors of the rainbow. Is this not like the variegated, colorful life I have built for myself, mixing cultures and new experiences while sweeping away much of the past conditioning?

I digress to tell you about building our house in Costa Rica. People ask, "Wasn't that difficult?" I don't see it as any more difficult than building a house anywhere, but one example was far from ordinary.

We came up with about 35 concepts, mostly integrating our house into the surroundings as much as possible, the most vital aspect being able to see the ocean. Wes met with the builder, going over each detail of the design. He came home briefly before leaving for the Republic of Georgia. "Are you sure the builder got it all? He does not always listen." "Oh yes, I stood on a ladder and showed him everything."

A few days later, I was in our home in Virginia. I clearly "heard" an inner voice, *They are building the house backward.* What could I do? Wes was not available via the Internet and I didn't know the builder's number. At the exact time in Georgia, due to time zones, Wes was having a nightmare. He was in a U-shaped foundation, (our house is U-shaped) experiencing some kind of violence. He had to abandon the foundation. He woke in a sweat.

Wes decided to see if the Internet was working. By some miracle it was and there was an email from our builder, "Call me as soon as possible and have your house plans." Wes thought he would wait because he didn't have our house plans with him, but something made him decide to try the builder in Costa Rica. It was about 8:30 p.m. in Costa Rica. He spoke with the builder and sure enough, they were building the house backward. They were going to put the walls up the next day and we would have not had our dream house. They had to take up the foundation and start over, just as in the dream. Even though we were not in Costa Rica at the time, its peaceful impact opened us to hear what normally might have been lost.

Just as we have swept our conditioning into memories, I watched the monks sweep the past, the beautiful mandala, away in an instant. They handed me a tiny bag of sand (memories) to take with me and off I went. I cannot say our move to Costa Rica has come with that ease — trust when fear of the unknown is grasping our thoughts. Still, the image inspires my adjustment.

How did we decide to buy here to start with? Hardly a decision, it was more like the joy of receiving a new jigsaw puzzle. We were fairly new in our relationship. The excitement of a shiny new adventure, putting irregular pieces together to compose our history seemed romantic. At the same time fitting each piece together in retrospect was haphazard. Only after 10 years do we really feel how right the pieces fit to give us a life in a new country.

We both had previously visited Costa Rica, enjoying its peaceful, friendly lushness. A friend told me about some property he had bought that was doubling or tripling in value. So off on vacation we went. The property turned out to be nothing we would ever live on so we could not buy and then sell it in good conscience.

We were referred to a couple of other American developers but their ethics and ours did not fit. Anyway, we were only exploring, right? Somehow we found ourselves driving for miles on dusty, pot-holed roads as someone had told us, "Go south young man." There were few houses — only cowboys, fields and mountains visible. I was furiously exclaiming, "Why don't you turn around, I would never live here!" I am not exactly a city girl but I do love lots of interactions with family and friends.

Live here?! How did that even get into the conversation?

Suddenly after hours we landed smack dab on a gorgeous, apparently isolated beach. As a beach lover from childhood I was mesmerized by the sparkling blue thundering waves, black sand and pure spaciousness. I jumped out of the car and ran down the empty beach.

I noticed off to the side stood a beach shack with a sign, "Come watch the Super Bowl here." Huh? I thought we were in outer space.

The contradictions of Costa Rica had started their subtle seduction of our souls.

The surfer dude in the beach shack looked up curiously. We told him our story. He immediately referred us back up the road to his friend Ben. Ben, a handsome landscape architect from California, soon greeted us. As he showed us around the development, certain words jumped into place in our puzzle. "Preserve monkey paths." "Have lots of green areas." "We want a sense of community." I was hooked.

The infrastructure was in place. The builders, developers and Ben all had bought lots. This was reassuring. Talk about spontaneity, within two days, risk-takers that we are, we had signed the papers.

That was 10 years ago. We both continued to work, taking longer and longer vacations in Costa Rica. Gradually we built our "vacation home." We rented it out as, a dream come true, we wanted to share it with friends when we were not there. While it paid our expenses, damages kept occurring.

We started working on getting Costa Rican residency, dealing with the bureaucracy. What happened to the smiling, gentle folks we were expecting? But we did it. Somehow almost unconsciously we decided to live our dream.

Back in Virginia, clarity struck. In a simple life, there is little sense in keeping our house or most of our belongings. Thus started five months of decision-making to get rid of lifelong *stuff*. Five months of sadness amidst an exchange of responsibility for freedom. Five months of seeing the joy in the faces of friends when I gifted them with items chosen especially for them. Our house sold in two days for more than we asked. More relief and loss to bring us the simple happiness we feel here.

The contradictions continue to draw me. I love walking down dirt roads to the beach as I did as a child in New England. I love the lack of stores, theaters, writing groups and all the cultural mandates. I miss the shopping, theater and proximity of family. I look forward to understanding more of the *tico* culture, including the unending patience and acceptance when the water is turned off, lines at the health clinic extending around the block, and travel delays caused by huge ruts or herds of cattle in the middle of the road.

We are in our early 70s. Our energy is not quite what it used to be. Will we be in our house, the house we designed with such love, forever? We live moment to moment now, knowing no one can predict how circumstances might change our decisions. For today, we look out at our fruit orchard, enjoy our privacy, listen to the waves, see the thousands of stars twinkling their approval, and sigh in gratitude. Grateful for the abundance we could not afford in the states, grateful for the friendly openness of the *ticos*.

I shudder at my struggle to learn Spanish but am determined to succeed. My respectful connections to a new culture will also hopefully keep alive some dying brain cells as they strain to learn something new.

This is our opportunity after a lifetime of hard work to sit back and just *be* in a country that values nature, peace and warmth as my husband and I do. The pieces of our life's puzzle are slowly creating a picture.

Wes worked in International Finance after the Peace Corps. He has lived all over the world, thus has the most patience with systems. I have moved from place to place since childhood, sometimes traumatically. My DNA actually says I am from a tribe in Africa called the Travelers! As an adult I trained in clinical social work, and had a fascination for people of all walks of life from an early age. We are outside-the-box folks. We are not chained to the cultural conditioning as many of our friends are. This entails both personal advantages and sacrifices. It is not easy for me to be far from family and life friends. Sometimes I wonder if we are selfish to live our dream. Other times I am more in touch with gratitude for the basic simplicity of life after a lifetime of hard work.

While we are not political refugees as some we have met, we do find the politics in Costa Rica more in line with our ideals. To live amidst such poverty can be difficult although I envy the joyful ease of life. I sometimes feel overwhelmed and resort to my spiritual mind view of doing what I can, connecting with love. Soon we will go for our drivers' licenses. "Why do we need a blood test?" Wes questions. What other country cares for its citizens by preparing ahead in case of an accident? Then again, is this a reality-based function in view of some of the driving habits? I am fearful of driving on city streets as the lanes are disorganized and drivers are aggressive. Eventually my courage will surmount this. I look forward to experiencing the bus too.

We both have a curiosity about other cultures; we are not tourists when we travel. Thus, we have gained a higher tolerance than most for anomalies. Most members of our families live a mere 20 miles from their birthplace.

We have many plans for the future, both here and around the world. For now, my health issues have changed some of them. A diagnosis of celiac disease suddenly put brakes on my lifelong joy of eating. I am grateful for Costa Rica's fresh fruits and vegetables, experimenting with yucca, lychee fruit and more.

Soon I will be hosting a writers workshop with old friends excited about visiting from the states. Wes is sponsoring a cross-Costa Rica bike trip with equally excited friends. Our framework will be a couple of months in California with a grandchild, a couple of months in Pennsylvania/Massachusetts with other family including two great grandchildren, and home to Costa Rica. Loved ones tug at my heart while the tranquility of Costa Rica tugs back. My psyche is adjusting, sometimes painstakingly, to this puzzle piece of a life in Costa Rica. Dreams do come true. Maybe not in the way we imagine. Our adventures continue, we thrive, balancing peace with figuring out the bureaucracy puzzle. The pieces slowly come together. For now, for today, we are grateful for how the pieces are meshing. The future is as impermanent as the monks' mandalas. Costa Rica's slow beauty comforts us. Will the frustrations ever outweigh the beauty? Only time will tell, one day at a time.

Judith Donovan
Age 75
US / Costa Rica

Judith Donovan is a retired clinical social worker. She currently spends most of the year in Costa Rica. However, the joy of family which now includes five great-grandchildren, draws her back to various parts of the United States each year. Judith is appreciating her free time in retirement to write her memoir plus extensive travel experiences, most recently to Nepal. She is also a dedicated meditator of many years, mentoring others.

"Twenty years from now you will be more disappointed by the things you didn't do than by the ones you did do. So throw off the bowlines, sail away from the safe harbor. Catch the trade winds in your sails. Explore. Dream. Discover."

— Mark Twain

A Shattered Field of Dreams?

Alvin Starkman, M.A., J.D.

I see you less now than when you were working, my wife has occasionally exclaimed since we "retired" from Toronto to Oaxaca about 12 years ago. Oaxaca, a UNESCO World Heritage Site in south-central Mexico, is best known for its exquisite colonial architecture and Dominican churches, quaint cobblestone downtown streets, its zócalo, or central square, museums, the best cuisine in the country, and being less than an hour's drive from myriad craft villages, pre-Hispanic Zapotec ruins, and artisanal production facilities of the country's iconic agave-based spirit, mezcal.

But the major draw for us was not one of those attractions, not even the year-round agreeable weather or extremely affordable cost of living; it was the people. Almost immediately after we began regularly vacationing in Oaxaca in 1991, we started to make friends, both middle-class urban Oaxacans of Spanish descent and mixed-heritage and rural folk of much more modest means, mainly Zapotec natives with rich and diverse cultural traditions and Spanish as their second language. In both cases we were warmly welcomed into their homes and lives and encouraged to attend, and at times participate in, occasions marking rites of passage, celebrating births and mourning deaths, being honored with requests to be godparents at weddings and quince años (coming of age religious rituals and festivities for 15-year-old female adolescents), baptisms, first communions, annual village fiestas and more.

I had been a lawyer, my wife a psychotherapist. After the first 10 years of practicing law, I began to dislike the life of a family law litigator despite the financial rewards. We gradually began vacationing more and more in Oaxaca, at first once a year for 10 days or so, then twice annually when we could get away. Before the "big move" in 2004, the pattern was traveling to Oaxaca three times a year for never less than two nor more than six weeks at a time. Frequent visits were not enough. The yearning to return enveloped us those 10 months a year we were living and working in Toronto. We knew we were destined to end up in Oaxaca but couldn't wait until the "proper time" for retirement. We consulted our financial advisor, and he confirmed we could probably afford to do it. I would be 53 and my wife 56.

We bought a piece of land in a semi-rural suburb of Oaxaca, and then by long distance, mainly through phoning and faxing our architect/project manager, spent four years building what is still for us our dream home — something we never could have afforded to do in Toronto, or for that matter anywhere in Canada or the US. We deferred moving into our new casa until our daughter had completed high school. We sold our Toronto home, I sold my half of the law practice to my partner, and our daughter entered university residence. We finally high-tailed it out of Dodge and moved permanently to Oaxaca. By that time we had as many friends in Oaxaca as we did in Toronto, making for a smooth and easy transition.

Learning the language made a huge difference for us. We each had some Spanish in our former lives, me in first-year university, and my wife throughout high school in Chicago. Our social lives were not restricted to hanging out with other expats. Twice during our years of frequent visits to Oaxaca we took intensive Spanish language courses, each of us one on one with our own instructor, four hours a day, five days a week. The first time it was for a month and then several months later for two weeks. That raised us to a level where we felt comfortable conversing and enabled us to more easily make friends.

Moving when we did was nevertheless somewhat of a precipitous decision for two reasons. First, our daughter was only 17 years old at the time, and as it turned out suffered separation anxiety for the first couple of years of college back in Canada. She lost a year but fortunately overcame it and has turned out fine, college degree, stable employment and all. Second, we had no idea how we would pass our time in our new homeland. My wife had taken a course certifying her to teach English as a second language, which she now does a few hours a week together with providing psychotherapy to the odd neurotic expat and a couple of Oaxacans. I assumed that I would turn into a fat old drunk, daily sitting in my favorite rocker on the terrace listening to rock music. You can do that only for so long, as much as I tried to retard reality. Thankfully I learned it rather quickly.

We had built our home with a guest level, anticipating that friends and family would want to visit regularly. Who knew that after a first visit, two at the most, our loved ones would realize they could have an all-inclusive Mexican vacation, airfare included, in Cancun, Puerto Vallarta or Huatulco, for less than the cost of flights alone to visit us in Mexico's interior — with not a beach in sight or margarita in hand? ("Mezcal? No way. I used to eat that worm in college and get drunk as a skunk. You're not getting me to try that again. Now I can afford single malt scotch.")

Damned Kevin Kostner and W.P. Kinsella: if you build it, the fact is that they'll only come once or twice. Our field of dreams shattered, we decided to rent out the guest level as a bed and breakfast of sorts. Part of the house had been roughed in for a second kitchen with water for a sink and a propane connection for a stove. But we resolved that we were not going to make breakfast for strangers in our semi-golden years, so we made the lower level of our home a self-contained, two-bedroom apartment, including full kitchen, washroom and private patio. Our guests would make their own breakfasts and come and go using their own entrance. Now this was more palatable.

We joined the local Oaxaca Bed & Breakfast Association and were in business, renting out part of our house most of the year for a week or more at a time. We enjoyed hosting tourists. Our guests were taking guided tours to the sights and places my wife and I had visited umpteen times. Heck, why not take them to those places on our own, and better yet to places tourists rarely got to see? Our world was Oaxaca, and we could show people what "the real Mexico" was all about by avoiding some of the regular tourist attractions and traps. Now that was providing value-added service.

But living in the real Mexico, at least in Oaxaca, and for the first time experiencing the life of a resident rather than as a frequent visitor meant having to make several significant adjustments: drinking only bottled water; putting all soiled toilet paper in the trash can rather than flushing it; learning that when someone, whether a retailer or a tradesperson, promised something in "quince dias" (two weeks), it usually meant much longer, even months; getting used to hour-long lineups at the bank; twice weekly for the first year having to hop in the pickup with all our garbage and track down the garbage truck; learning the ropes concerning medical care and how to negotiate between private doctors and hospitals and our Mexican national health insurance plan coverage. But we made them and gradually life became routine.

One day I received an email from a professor at Toronto's York University, my old alma mater. He was teaching an e-marketing course, and looking for small Internet-based businesses. He would divide his class into groups of three or four and ask each to do a major term paper, analyzing a small business like our B&B and preparing a final report; what the enterprise was doing right and wrong and how could it improve.

Six months later I received a 25-page analysis of Casa Machaya Oaxaca Bed & Breakfast. I understood very little of what was in it, having been, and still being rather technologically simple. But I did understand the part where the students suggested that I begin writing articles about Oaxaca in order to increase our Internet presence. Just a short bio at the end of each article which included the name of our bed and breakfast would help our search engine ranking. With two social anthropology degrees to my credit, and having spent my waking hours as a lawyer drafting pleadings, affidavits and factums, I knew how to write. Furthermore, I had already been writing a bi-monthly column, "Legally Speaking", for a Canadian national antiques and art magazine.

I became a more serious writer, publishing on as many websites as possible, as well as writing for print magazines and newspapers every sort of article about Oaxaca — its craft villages and multiplicity of ethno-linguistic groups, artist and artisan profiles, cooking school and restaurant reviews, and whatever other diverse aspect of life in Southern Mexico I could imagine and then muster. With online access to recent Canadian cases touching on antiques and art, I continued to write my legal column. I would not permit my legal mind to atrophy.

The federal government caught wind of my ramblings and thought I would be an asset to a new program designed to promote tourism and investment in Mexico. So the feds hired me. And I loved it. After having written over 200 articles and received virtually no direct compensation for my efforts, here came Mexico's federal government wanting to pay me to become a part of *Mexico Today: Marca País, Imagen de México*. My contracts stated that I had to not only write but also be active on social media. So I learned about Facebook, Twitter and LinkedIn. By the time the federal gigs had ended, I had become hooked on social media.

B&B proprietor, showing friends and other house guests the sights in and around Oaxaca, writer and journalist, and now obsessed with social media — yes, I guess my wife was right about my working hours. However, I was able to sleep through the entire night as contrasted with my former life as a litigator when I woke up two or three times a week in the middle of the night worrying about what I had forgotten to ask the day before when cross-examining a client's estranged spouse, or whether there was enough money in the account to pay the firm's staff. I had also begun writing about Oaxacan charities, the ones I felt were totally transparent and doing an admirable job helping needy residents of the state, mainly with regard to education and health care. One thing led to another, and before I knew it I was spending a fair bit of time supporting select charities through participating in fundraising events and writing about them to help raise their profiles.

One day I received an email from a Canadian snowbird who asked if I would be interested in becoming a director of www.canfro.ca, a registered Canadian charity for the benefit of worthy Oaxacan causes. There were no Canadians on the Board of Directors who were full-time residents of Oaxaca, and the charity needed one in order to best administer funds. I offered to participate, but only if CANFRO (Canadian Friends of Oaxaca Inc.) supported the two causes most dear to me. The directors voted, and I became vice-president. I had begun drinking mezcal in the early 1990s when we began our regular visits to Oaxaca. The spirit intrigued me, so I began to learn about its origins, production methods, and innumerable nuances. I wrote an article about mezcal, a primer to help travelers to Oaxaca who were similarly curious and wanted to learn more. Then I wrote another article, and another. I began exploring the farthest reaches of Oaxaca's central valleys and beyond, learning about differing traditions relating to the production of mezcal, and about the history and lifestyles of its makers, the *palenqueros* as they're known in the state of Oaxaca. I became impressed with the sustainability of the industry and began investigating that aspect and then writing about the interrelationship of mezcal, agave and sustainability.

Oaxacan tour companies take visitors along routes into the hinterland to see the sights. Most include as an option a visit to an artisanal mezcal distillery. But by and large travelers are taken to facilities built for the tourist trade and not to *palenques* off the beaten track which exist to supply Oaxacans rather than visitors to the state. I had found a(nother) niche for myself, taking mezcal aficionados, bar and restaurant owners and their staffs, and prospective exporters of the spirit to learn about mezcal on full-day excursions. No one was doing that despite the rising popularity of mezcal worldwide.

Mezcal Educational Excursions of Oaxaca, a registered trademark with the federal government, was born. I obtained a tax number since I would now be earning money from one of my ventures. I informed our bed and breakfast accountant that he had a new client. I also had to get permission from the department of immigration, which I did, to enable me to teach about the culture of mezcal and pre-Hispanic fermented beverages such as *pulque* and *tepache.*

I created a bilingual mezcal tasting wheel together with a *palenquero* friend. He then encouraged me to write a book about the spirit's complexity and nuances, so that became my next project. Both publications have been warmly welcomed by bookstores, mezcalerías and gift shops in Oaxaca, with sales higher than expected. In the course of promoting mezcal, I've done book signings in Oaxaca and Toronto. All I ever wanted to do was promote mezcal locally and recoup my investment from both projects.

Around the time the mezcal seed began to germinate, my wife and I were becoming tired of running Casa Machaya Oaxaca Bed & Breakfast. This was supposed to be fun and relaxing, a way to help travelers to Oaxaca, not feel like work; remember, we are retired. Apparently the average time B&Bs exist is seven years. We were on our way to paying our dues. In addition, some of my wife's energy had been zapped as a result of having had three hip replacement surgeries in less than a year.

Our favorite goddaughter from a small village over an hour's drive from Oaxaca had been accepted to a private medical school in the city. We decided to invite her to live with us for the duration of her higher education and occupy the apartment which had been the B&B. We decided that the cost of her medical school education would be our responsibility. It had to be, given the extremely modest means of her family. The

B&B income had looked after her high school education already. Medical school is another story of course, but me taking mezcal aficionados on distillery tours goes a long way towards covering tuition, books and living expenses. Whether at the end of the day it does or does not fully cover her costs, we're in for the long haul, from our hearts.

A dozen years ago, in my wildest dreams I could not have imagined that this is what retirement would look like for us. No bridge club, no tennis, no art classes — for either of us. My wife loves her gardening and is an avid reader. Our social lives are filled, daily if we want, visiting with friends both in Oaxaca and throughout its central valleys, going to downtown gallery exhibit inaugurations and restaurant openings; and for me, at least right now, teaching, writing about, and otherwise promoting mezcal. We've both learned to not look too far into the future, since no doubt a decade from now our retirement will be vastly different from what it is today. And with a little gentle persuasion exerted towards our goddaughter, we might have a gerontologist in the family to look after our medical needs.

Alvin Starkman
Age 64
Canada / Oaxaca, Mexico

Alvin Starkman operates Mezcal Educational Excursions of Oaxaca. He is the author of Mezcal in the Global Spirits Market: Unrivalled Complexity, Innumerable Nuances.

Musings from the Monastery

By Earl Goodson

Why?
"Why?" has been the question my life has revolved around. I still can't answer it fully, but I think I can give it a shot on the subject of travel. I'm living in New Zealand, just outside the Auckland area. There's a number of Buddhist temples and a few monasteries as well, and I'm the Caretaker of Vimutti Buddhist Monastery for a second year. I've done a lot of traveling in my expat years but it's never been entirely consistent. New Zealand was my first international living experience and I consider it dipping my toe into international waters, relatively speaking. New Zealand is certainly not the United States, my home country, but compared to say, Honduras, you could be forgiven for thinking you hadn't just spent 12 hours on a plane crossing the Pacific.

Wanderlust and adventure first drove me to look abroad for a job opportunity in 2009. And it was absolute good fortune that I happened upon this job listing for a Monastic Caretaker on Craigslist one day. After finding the advert, I spent a great deal of time getting excited about the position, followed by a short amount of time telling myself it was almost certainly a scam and even if it weren't, it was a month old and probably already filled and I shouldn't get so excited, but did anyways. The very next day I received an email: "Greetings from Vimutti Monastery. We'd like to know why you wish to apply for the position of Caretaker."

"The monks start their day with soy milk offered by hand before their devotional chanting and meditation and I don't want to be late with it."

Well. I got right down to brass tacks and wrote a rather verbose description of my love for horticulture and nature (I was just finishing a term doing trail maintenance and construction through Americorps), my fascination with religion of all stripes, my love for travel and desire for an international experience and though not a Buddhist I'd always wanted to learn meditative practice. And Ajahn Chandako wrote back saying, "We like what we see. If you can get here, you've got the job!" I paraphrase slightly but that's the gist. So I sold as much as I could, getting all I owned down to one backpack, and flew across the world. I've done that several times now and my backpack grows a bit then shrinks dramatically each time I do so. It feels good to de-clutter, de-complicate things.

At the end of 2008 I spent a year in one of the most beautiful countries on Earth, a country the same size as Colorado only far more diverse in character. World-class subtropical beaches, mountain ranges, forest trails, volcanoes, sub-Antarctic islands, charming small towns, a stunning metropolis (yes, I do say "a"; New Zealand is a country of towns and small cities), and the best skies on the planet. I got to know the quirky English (as if my Americanized Anglicisms were any different to their ears) and even stole a few terms. One of my Texan high school students accused me of faking "cheers" whenever I say "thank you" to sound "international," but my brain really did annex that on its own, I swear. (I also say "Aiya!" whenever I drop something, but that's another story).

I returned briefly in 2012 and again at the end of 2014 because of the lifestyle. Since I left the monastery, I've done my absolute best to live a life and be a person in the world and haven't done a very good job of it. Too much work and too many questions — I think the monks knew what they were doing when they invited me and now I'm addicted. Meditation is the "why?" of everything and it needs more of my attention these days. Having a place where I don't have to worry about rent, food is provided (if only once a day), Internet distractions are mercifully far (I have an addiction) and I can have a staring contest with a tree is indeed a blessing. That tree shares my nature and sitting in Nature, I find I already know the answer to "why" if I stop and listen. It's a diverse life as well — some days I'm running a chainsaw chasing down invasive barberry and willows on our 125 acres. Others I'm cutting trail and laying gravel on new walking paths. Maybe another day I'm receiving guests and visiting monks from Thailand and preparing ceremonial incense and flower offerings. Maybe I have the day off and I can smell the rain drumming on my forest kuti. And maybe one day I won't need an answer to "Why?" There will just be This.

I awaken one day and the sun has yet to crest the horizon. The morning fog has yet to burn off and the wind is scented lightly with pine and dew. Today's sunrise is a buttery gold color pouring between the black silhouettes of the trees — how is it the same palette looks so radically different each day? The sheep are talking to each other in the next pasture and hopefully the makeshift patches I put together on the fencing will keep them on the proper side. I have a bag full of cartons of soy milk. The monks start their day with soy milk offered by hand before their devotional chanting and meditation and I don't want to be late with it. Walking down the gravel path, the chill is already starting to fade. One breath in. A bird heralds the arrival of the new day. One breath out. A bee busily coasts by, sparing me not the slightest mind. And so my day begins, breath by breath, step by step.

By step...By car trip...By plane trip...By new apartment...By new job.

Now I find myself in Taiwan, holding the wisps of a green memory in my hands. I could say it was time to move on. I could say I was ready to re-tackle the outside world. I could own up to the wanderlust that defines many expats. But who really knows? Stillness is here, in Taipei, much as it is in the pine groves of New Zealand. I will return and I will go, but home is wherever I can find a moment to be still and ask "Why?" Finding one's place anywhere and nowhere is a double-edged sword in a world seemingly content with stone niches. I have my backpack. And the breath. And so a new day begins, breath by breath, step by step.

Earl Goodson
Age 32
US / New Zealand / Taipei, Taiwan

Earl is an aspiring travel writer and photographer who follows the wind and his heart to find love and joy in the ordinary as much as the extraordinary. Websites: earlgoodson.smugmug. com, turbotroll.wordpress.com

Expat Resources

Association of Americans Resident Overseas: aaro.org

AARO is an international, nonpartisan association with members in 46 countries.

Easy Expat: easyexpat.com

Provides expats with accurate information and answers about the major cities with the most expatriates.

Escape Artist: escapeartist.com

Empowers individuals to live their dream to live, work, play, retire or invest in a country of their choice.

Expat Blog: expatsblog.com

Website featuring several blogs written by expats.

Expat Exchange: escapeartist.com

Among the first sites dedicated to expatriates and their specific needs.

Expat Explorer Survey: expatexplorer.hsbc.com

The Expat Explorer survey, now in its eighth year, is one of the largest independent global expat surveys.

Expat Focus: expatfocus.com

Information portal offering news, information and advice for expats across the world.

Expat Media Hub: expatmediahub.com

A worldwide directory of on and offline media and content for those living outside their country of origin.

Expat Network: expatnetwork.com

An online resource for expats living and working abroad. Highlights include a job board and forum.

The Expat Survey: theexpatsurvey.com

The aim of the project is to gain a true understanding of expatriate life across all nationalities and territories.

Transitions Abroad: transitionsabroad.com

Resources for expats living, working, studying and volunteering abroad, existing for 30 years.

InterNations: internations.org

An international online community that connects expats worldwide.

Wall Street Journal Expat: blogs.wsj.com/expat

"Expat" is The Wall Street Journal's hub for expatriates and global nomads.

Made in the USA
Monee, IL
20 November 2021